Amityville

My Sister's Keeper

A Story of Death, Deception and the Occult

Micky Sexton

Darby Press

Louisville, KY

DARBY PRESS

Darby Press, PO Box 768, Simpsonville, KY 40067

This story is based on my memories and records kept over the years. In some cases, names and locations have been changed to protect those who are not central to this memoir. This story is based on my recollections, memories, notes, and other documentation as accurately as the memory will allow.

Names: Sexton, Micky, author.
Title: Amityville - my sister's keeper : a story of death , deception , and the occult / Micky Sexton.
Description: Louisville, KY: Darby Press, 2016.
Identifiers: ISBN 978-0-9966474-6-5 | 978-0-9966474-7-2 (e-book).
Subjects: LCSH Sexton, Micky. | Lutz, George Lee. | Lutz, Kathleen. | Demonology. | Satanism. | Occultism. | Occultists. | Parapsychology--New York (State)--Amityville. | Amityville (N.Y.)--Biography. | BISAC BODY, MIND & SPIRIT / Occultism | BODY, MIND & SPIRIT / Unexplained Phenomena | BIOGRAPHY / Rich and Famous.
Classification: LCC BF1517.U6 S49 2016 | 133.4/2--dc23

introduction

My name is Micky Sexton. In 1977, Jay Anson wrote a book called the *Amityville Horror*. It told the story of George Lee Lutz and his wife Kathy Lutz and their 28-day stay in the "Amityville House." According to the Lutz's, the Amityville house was haunted. After 28 days, they moved out, never to return. For years, there has been speculation that the "haunting" of the Amityville house was a hoax. *Amityville Horror* sold millions of copies and the central story has been the focus of many spin-off movies, interviews, documentaries and docudramas. Until now, the real story of George and Kathy Lutz remains untold.

Kathy Lutz was my sister. George Lee Lutz was my brother-in-law. When Kathy married George Lutz, she had three children from a previous marriage. Those children, Daniel, Christopher, and Melissa are my nephews and niece. I babysat the children from the time of their births.

This book chronicles Kathy's relationship with Lutz. My sister's marriage affected all of us. This book tells the "story behind the story." It is my account, told in my own words of the horror that began the day my sister met George Lee Lutz.

I have been a silent witness. Keeping my secret and my story for forty years. Many of us have encountered evil people in our lives. George Lee Lutz was one of the most evil men that I have ever known and the only one I deemed to be a true *warlock*.

My sister met Lee long before they moved into the Amityville house. Within hours of meeting "Lee," my sister was a changed woman. Her metamorphosis took less than twenty-four hours—hair, makeup, even language. She began to curse more frequently, with more intensity—more hateful. I believe George Lee Lutz indoctrinated my sister into the occult. I remember the night that he held a meeting of witches, a coven, to usher my sister into the occult. I was babysitting my niece and nephews that night.

Over the years, many people have suspected that Lutz was involved with the occult. I saw many occult practices surrounding Lee. I saw animal abuse, drugging people, casting spells, mind control, and levitation. The events I describe in the book are true as I saw them. Although memories may fade with time, the conversations recounted in the book are as I remember.

Days after their relationship began; it became clear to me that Lutz was drugging my sister and her children. This unforgivable practice began before they moved into the Amityville house and continued until my sister divorced George, ending their eleven-year marriage.

After living in the Amityville house for only 28 days, Kathy and Lee moved out. The story widely reported was that they moved because of "paranormal" activity. According to their recorded interviews, the family fled to be free from the "spirits" that inhabited the house. After leaving the Amityville house, they moved into my mother's home in West Babylon, NY, where the warlock continued his hoax.

During their stay with my mother and me, I saw George use intimidation, manipulation, and mind-control on family and visitors.

If you have never had experience with the occult, I can assure you. It is real. Although dealing with the occult is daunting, it is not hopeless. I was born and raised to believe in God.

Discernment is a "a gift of the spirit." According to the Bible, a person operating with discernment can *see* demons and angels. They can also discern the *spirit* of individuals.

Through the gift of discernment, I was able to save my life and avoid the worst effects of the warlock's witchcraft, rage, and curses.

In 1981, George Lee Lutz would *murder* me with a curse, but the Lord brought me back. This book is about those events that culminated in the destruction of the

peace of mind and health of my sister and unforgettable
pain and heartache for me and my family.

Micky Sexton

CHAPTER ONE

the early days

I grew up in a modest neighborhood in Long Island, New York, about five miles as the crow files, from that infamous place known as the "Amityville House." My sister Kathy and I grew up in a modest ranch-style home with four bedrooms and a partially finished basement. The rooms were small, but we had what we needed. I never imagined that my sister would divorce her high-school sweetheart and marry a warlock.

Kathy, was born when Mom was only seventeen. She and Dad were both young but excited to have a new baby. My sister and I were on the leading edge of what the kids today call "the hippie generation." Kathy was born in 1946. Two years later, my brother Jimmy was born, then Joan and finally me—the baby. My parents christened me "Mildred Patricia Conners," but the first day Mom brought me home from the hospital, Kathy, who was ten years older, nicknamed me "Micky."

"Mom she looks like a 'Micky' to me. Can we call her Micky?" Kathy was adamant, and the name stuck. From that day on, I was "Micky." Later in life, I would have my first name legally changed to Micky.

There were loads of kids in our Long Island neighborhood, mostly German-Irish. My family and most of my neighbors where of Irish descent. I was a "ginger head" from day one ... or so my Mom told me.

The houses filled with Italian immigrants lined the streets of my childhood. I remember even as a tiny child, I could close my eyes as I walked outside and know what part of the block I was walking in by the wonderful cooking aromas that lofted into the street. It was an international cacophony of smells.

There were great and wonderful things about living in an ethnic neighborhood. The great smells of talented wives who were master chefs in their own homes. There were always people around and never a shortage of playmates. Everything I ever wanted or needed, I could find within a five-block radius of my house. However, there were also some not-so-great things. It was the 1950s and I understood that the Italian "mob" ruled the neighborhood. They owned all of the major businesses, including the super market, bowling alley, roller rink, pizzeria, and of course, all of the bars. If you were doing business in our neighborhood, your business was controlled, or owned by the Italian mob. As a child, I perceived this situation as benign. It was not good or bad, it just "was."

Because she was older, my sister Kathy often took care of me while Mom worked in Syosset at Grumman's Aerospace. Dad liked to drink, and gamble so he was not always around. As my siblings and I got older, Dad was around less, until finally he was not around at all. We heard from him from time to time, but he had his own life to live, and that life, most of the time, did not include us.

Kathy was my surrogate mother, but it did not feel awkward to me. I was glad. God knows Mom was too tired when she got home to be worried with all of us kids.

Johanna was my mother's name, although everyone called her "Joan." She was quiet and reserved. A private woman, she believed in modesty in all things: dress, makeup, hair, clothing, and behavior. She wore no makeup save a light, well-blotted coating of lipstick. She would paint her lips, then take a tissue and blot most of the color away. I can still see the lipstick marks on that white tissue. Her auburn hair was thick and slightly curly. I got my red hair from her.

Each morning she would dress quickly, apply her lipstick, give her hair a vigorous brush, and leave for work. She took her work seriously and was dedicated to her job—she never missed a day. Growing up with her was like growing up with a reliable caretaker. She covered all the necessary things for life: food, shelter, clothing; but she never talked with us—not really. Mom was always reserved and careful about what she said to us. However, when she wanted to make a point, all eyes and ears turned to her. She made sure we "got it."

I remember one time, telling her that I was sick to my stomach, and needed to stay home from school for the day. She looked at me, and gave me that Mom-look of disapproval."

"Mick, why are you lagging behind today? I need to get to work ... make it snappy. Come on now! If you insist on staying home, you have to stay in bed, no playing outside ... no talking on the phone. Got it?" I "got it," but I hated it.

Mom never missed work, but she was married to an abusive husband. My father drank. He drank a lot when he came home. Then he would get mean. He loved to take that meanness out on my mother and on us. The entire neighborhood knew it. My father had a reputation of being a bully. After twenty-three years of "taking it," Mom divorced him. He moved out and they never got back together.

After the divorce, she loved having her own life. She never re-married; she could not risk being controlled by a man again. To this day, I believe that watching Mom live with such a controlling man helped lead Kathy, later in life, to marry the same type of man.

I was no different than my siblings ... we all wore our scars from those years.

When we were growing up, occasionally a catalog book would come to the house from Montgomery Ward or Sears. That was always an exciting day. We called them "dream books." I watched as Kathy poured over the catalog with one of her friends or perhaps with a neighbor who stopped by for a cup of coffee.

I could not wait until they left the house so I could lay down on the floor and spread the catalog open in front of me. I would pour through the pages: toys, furniture, bedspreads, dishes, jewelry, make-up, television sets—it was like a dream. Minutes would fly as I dreamed of having my own jewelry box with a beautiful ballerina, or a soft plush teddy bear for my bed.

One day, after Kathy and one of her friends had spent the afternoon looking at makeup in the dreambook, she and her friend disappeared into the bathroom. From the safety of the bathroom doorway, I watched in fascination as the two girls plucked their eyebrows bald, then drew a dark arching line above their eyes with an eyebrow pencil. To me, it gave their faces a hard, artificial look, but Kathy thought it was beautiful and classy, "just like a Hollywood actress."

Kathy was a beautiful girl with a great figure. In those days, she wore her hair in a huge puffy swoop, heavily sprayed. They called it a "beehive." It looked like one too. Once sprayed in place, it could last for days. I remember when I was in school one of the rumors going around was about two girls who had done their hair in stiffly sprayed beehive and weeks later, roaches had moved into their stationary locks. I never really believed it, but it sounded true.

Once my sister and her friend had finished drawing on their brows and stiffening their beehive, they were ready to complete the look with a pair of Capri pants and a shell-top. Shell-tops were a tight sleeveless sweaters made from polyester material and dyed in a pastel color. In those days, everything was made of polyester. Suits, dresses, pants, coats. It was hot and easily stained. The fabric did not breathe. It was like wearing a portable sauna. My dream was to be just like Kathy: beautiful, funny, and happy.

All decked out, hair sprayed within an inch of its life, and eyebrows carefully painted on, I watched the girls leave the house to go for a walk in the neighborhood. To me, they looked like the magazine models. They walked up the street as though they owned the block. I remember wishing I could be pretty like Kathy. I was seven and she was seventeen. She was so happy and carefree in those days. Too soon, her world and mine would change in a terrible way.

CHAPTER TWO

the break-up

Mom opened my bedroom door. "Micky," she said, "make sure that you are ready to leave in a few minutes. Your sister is coming to get you. She needs your help today." Kathy often picked me up to babysit or to help her clean. I could tell by the tone of Mom's voice that this was different. Something was wrong. That meant trouble of some kind, for me.

"Is something wrong Mom?"

"Well, you may as well know, Kathy and Seb have broken up. They are getting a divorce." Kathy had been married to her high-school sweetheart, Seb, for nine years.

"What?" I exclaimed.

"I am not going to discuss this right now, Micky. Just make sure you are ready to go when your sister gets here." Whenever Mom used my name in a sentence, I knew that she was annoyed. I went straight to my room and got dressed. It was a weekend, so I did not have to worry about anything. Once dressed, I went outside to sit on the steps and wait for Kathy. At seventeen, I was anxious to help my older sister who I idolized. I had no idea why she was leaving Seb. He had always been a nice person and he was, as far as I knew, a good husband and father. However, I thought that if Kathy was leaving him, he must have done something wrong.

Kathy and Seb were married in 1964, when I was eight years old and Kathy was eighteen. I think she always regretted not going to college, but in those days, most girls got married early and started a family. Seb and Kathy's married life had always been a huge part of my life. Seb was like a brother to me. The marriage had given Kathy three beautiful children. Danny was the oldest, Christopher was born next, and Melissa was the baby. When the kids were small, I was always the designated babysitter. I loved being "Aunt Micky," so I watched the kids whenever they needed me.

When Kathy pulled up in front of the house, I could see that she was angry. She turned into the driveway with force and screeched to a stop. The horn was blowing even though she could see me sitting on the front stoop. I could tell she was not getting out of the car. I jumped up, and hollered back to Mom, "I'll be back when Kathy and I are finished, Mom. I'm leaving." She did not acknowledge my call, but I knew she heard me.

"Hey, Mick, we're going to make a couple of extra stops before we head to my place. Okay?"

"Yeah, sure," I said. I was a little surprised at how my sister looked.

Kathy dressed with style. Her hair just so ... sprayed with hairspray so it would stay perfectly arranged. Today was different. Her Capri pants were wrinkled, her shirt untucked, and her picture-perfect hair askew.

She looked ragged and stressed, but I said nothing as I got into the car.

She was driving the Bonneville. A beautiful car. Seb was an excellent mechanic. He could build racecars. He always kept the family cars in pristine condition and running like the finest jet engines. The interior was immaculate. They were the stereotypical "beautiful couple." In high school, everyone thought Kathy and Seb would be together forever.

When I got into the car, Kathy said, "We're going to stop at the store for cardboard boxes." I assumed it was to pack her things and leave Seb. I said nothing. We passed right by the local grocery store, Zitos Market, where we bought candy and soft drinks when we were kids. I was surprised she had not stopped. I had walked to that market more times than I could count. So had Kathy. I asked her why she passed on getting the boxes from Zitos.

She laughed and said, "And let those jackasses know that my marriage is breaking up? You know how they are Mick; it will be all over the neighborhood by tomorrow.

It's none of their business." She drove on, headed for the big grocery on the main highway.

"The first thing I'm gonna do is get rid of all this *guinea-shit*," Kathy said with a frown on her face. I knew exactly what she meant. The Italian mob was an active force in the neighborhood. Since they owned all of the businesses, including Zitos, Kathy did not want to patronize the store anymore. In our neighborhood, especially in those days, some adults (especially when they were angry) would use the derogatory term "guineas" when referring to Italians. As a tiny child, I heard the expression all of the time. It was a term used with both fear and arrogance.

We stopped at the main grocery store and Kathy told me to come in with her so we could fill the car with empty boxes. The clerk had long, shaggy hair and an earring in each ear. "Have you got any extra boxes we can have?" Kathy asked.

"Yeah, sure. There're in the back of the store, take all you want."

"Come on Micky, let's go." Kathy was already out the front door and headed to the car. Behind the store was an overflowing dumpster with multiple cardboard boxes of all shapes and sizes. We began stuffing the back seat of the car and the trunk with boxes that read "Campbell's Soup" and "Kellogg's Frosted Flakes." I could see the embedded rings in the bottom of the cardboard, left from the weight of the soup cans.

Once the car was full, we drove to Kathy's house. She parked the car and walked in, yelling over her shoulder, "Bring the boxes inside, will ya, Mick?" It took me three trips to move all the boxes. When I brought in the last load, Kathy was standing in the living room, staring at the floor.

Kathy's house was a brick two-story, built in the '60s. It was a typical three-bedroom with a formal dining room and a small eat-in kitchen.

"Everything that I throw on the floor I want you to put into these boxes. When all the boxes are full, I want you to take them outside to the trash. I intend to get rid of all this junk."

"All this junk," I was sure she meant Seb's stuff, but I did not comment. Still red-faced, she began to jerk pictures from the walls, throwing them onto the floor as she went. Bam! Knick-knacks on the dresser crashed to the floor. Nothing within her reach was spared. Lamps, ashtrays, vases of all kinds landed on top of the growing piles. I quickly placed the loose items in the boxes. The living room finished, she made her way to the bedrooms.

I felt sorry for Seb. Kicked out of his own house. Most of his things thrown away or set on the curb.

Kathy tackled the master bedroom next. When she opened the master-bedroom door, I was amazed to see that the room was a mess. Kathy had always been a good homemaker and a neat-nik. "A place for everything, and everything in its place," she would say.

The dresser drawers gaped open. Articles of clothing spilled over the drawer walls. More clothes littered the floor and the closet doors were wide open. Only her clothes were hanging in the closet. Seb's clothing was gone. There was no sign that he had ever inhabited that room. We filled several boxes with her clothing, perfume bottles and makeup from her dresser top. She said something about "starting a new life," and that she "had to start fresh … out with the old and in with the new."

Next, we dealt with the kitchen. She immediately grabbed three pretty glass bowls she kept on the kitchen counter and put them into the empty cardboard box on the floor. "Those belonged to his mother," she said. "He can have em."

She opened and slammed shut each of the cupboards but removed nothing. When she was finished she said, "I'm going to be home all day so you don't have to watch the kids today. I'll let you know when I need you." She turned and walked out the door, headed toward the car. I followed. Kathy was unusually quiet. After a few minutes, I decided to take a chance and ask the question that had been burning in my heart all day.

"Kathy what happened between you and Seb? Why are you so upset? Why are you throwing away all of his things?"

She shot back, "He's been sleeping with another woman. That's all you need to know and don't you tell Mom—I don't want her to know." Kathy had always had a temper. Even when she was little, she was a spitfire. The kind who was not going to take crap from anyone.

Yet she had such a good heart. I think the moment was beginning to sink in: she was breaking up her marriage, with all the ramifications that would have for her and for her children. Lives are changing today, I thought to myself. I hope it is worth it in the end. It was a sobering moment for Kathy. A young woman who was soon to be on her own for the first time.

I wondered how the kids were doing. I was afraid to ask her where they were while we were cleaning out the house. How would a divorce affect them? They were children caught in the middle of a mess. What would be next? I got out of the car at Mom's house in silence.

***

Over the next few weeks, Seb moved his few remaining belongings out of the house and into his new apartment. Although Kathy had managed to throw away most of his things, he was able to salvage a few personal mementos.

Seb and Kathy had been married for nine years and their three children were happy kids in those days. When I would come over to babysit, they would play in the back yard with the other children from the neighborhood. Kathy's back yard was one of the favorite hangouts for all of the kids. While they played, I would cook dinner and when it got dark, they would come inside and eat, do their homework, and get ready for bed. If we had time, we would watch television for a while. They were happy, creative and playful. That ideal lifestyle was not going to last.

Something was on the horizon that would change everything. Soon, they would not be happy children, they would no longer be playful, or even communicative, and they would lose all semblance of "typical." None of us saw it coming, not Kathy, not me, not the kids … but he was coming. He was on the way … how could we have known?

CHAPTER THREE

transformation

Kathy had never worked outside of the home while she was married to Seb. Before they had married, Kathy had been a waitress. As a single mom, she had to go back to work. She took a job waiting tables at a local diner near her house. She needed help with the kids after school so she could work in the evenings. I was working the day shift at a local factory. I went in at six each morning and was off by two. Kathy would pick me up after work and drop me off in time to be there for the kids when they came home from school.

Over time, we worked out a good routine. The kids seemed to adjust to living without their dad around the house. Seb kept in touch with them on weekends, at least at first. That too would change but it was not Seb's fault. Kathy had never been an overly fussy mom, but instead preferred to let the kids handle what they could on their own. That had not changed with the divorce. She did not talk to the kids much about how they were "adjusting," she expected them to handle it. She was there for backup and support, if they needed it.

Kathy was happy and content. She liked her new waitress job. She had spent most of her adult life staying at home with the kids. She seemed to enjoy getting out and talking with customers.

Kathy took care of the kids during the day, and at night, when she left for work, I was there to watch them and make sure they got to bed on time.

***

One day in late summer, Kathy mentioned that she had met someone, a man that she found interesting. He was a surveyor and an ex-Marine. He would come by the diner almost every weeknight for dinner. Kathy told me he owned his own home and she thought his parents were "well-off." His surveying business was a three-generation business.

Although she never mentioned having a date or going to a movie with this person, she would tell me that "Lee" had stopped by the diner again. He would always sit at her table. I wondered if it might become a serious relationship. Kathy was like my mom, never one to discuss her personal life.

It was a beautiful day and I was thinking about letting the kids play outside that afternoon when Kathy pulled up in front of the factory. I thought someone else was driving her car. I stepped inside, took one look at my sister, and was dumbstruck. Astounded. In less than twenty-four hours, she had become someone I hardly recognized. She was wearing a pair of blue jeans paired with a small spaghetti-strapped summer top. I had never seen my sister in jeans. Her haircut was cut in a "shag" style and she was wearing long earrings. It was a total transformation.

Even her makeup was different. In the past, she had always worn makeup but it was never over-the-top. Today her eyes were raccooned with dark eyeliner, and her lips were red and glossy. I had never seen her look or dress this way. She was bubbling with excitement and seemed incredibly happy. Every other word was about "Lee."

Something had changed in their relationship. "Micky, I can't believe how handsome he is. He's beautiful!" She laughed as she said, "Mick, I smoked a joint with Lee last night. It was so much fun. He is so great. I love being with him." I could not believe my ears. My sister had never done drugs in her life. This was not like her. She giggled and said, "Mick, you would not believe how hung he is." She was right—I did not believe it. Who has kidnapped my sister and put this imposter in the car?

As a native New Yorker, Kathy spoke with her hands when she was excited and she was definitely excited today.

She had always been a lead-foot when it came to driving. She drove fast all the time, but today, she had one hand on the wheel and the other hand waving in the air as she described her new beau. As the car flew down the road, my mind raced. Kathy, the prim and proper one—so beautifully dressed. Her perfect hair. A talented seamstress. What is happening to my sister? I do not know this woman.

She could make anything with a sewing machine and routinely made beautiful clothing for herself and for her family: dresses for her, suits for her husband, and matching outfits for the kids. She had even designed her own sewing patterns and sold some of the designs to Vogue.

I thought about how many times she had ridiculed me for wearing blue jeans. She would say, "Is that all you can ever wear—jeans? You always have that cutoff look, your shirt tucked into a pair of jeans. Try something else. You look like a little hippie."

As we pulled into her driveway, Kathy suggested I spend the night. "I need you tomorrow to help me clean the house because Lee is coming over for dinner." As I walked up the stairs to go to bed, I had such a sense of dread. I had always had a "sixth-sense." Even as a child, I could feel and see things that others did not. I always thought of it as a spiritual gift from God, a discernment that came naturally to me. Many times in the past, I have had dreams or premonitions about family members or neighbors. I never shared them with anyone. Mom always thought that "second-sight," as she called it was, "a secret to be taken to the grave and never spoken about."

I climbed the steps to the spare bedroom. As I ascended, a wave of dread washed over me. Kathy's recent words and actions consumed my thoughts. Her changed appearance, smoking a joint, cursing and swearing, —all very different behaviors for my sister.

Even though Lee had been coming into the diner every day, they had only been talking for about two weeks. It concerned me that in only two weeks he had become so intimate with my sister. What is he trying to do?

Kathy told me that he had come to the diner for weeks without taking any notice of her. After some time, he began sitting at one of her tables every time he came in. He never said anything—just sat at one of her tables. Then two weeks ago, he had started talking to her, asking her questions. Kathy told me he wanted to know where she was "from" and if she was "married or had kids."

She said he had a "glimmer in his eye and a smile just for her." She was ecstatic with her newfound adorer. She wanted more—the change in her manner of dress reflected that. I got ready for bed, and soon fell asleep. My last thoughts were worrisome questions. *How has this man changed her so quickly? What power does he have over her and what is its source?*

The following morning, Kathy woke me early. "Before you start cleaning anything Mick, I need you to walk up to the store for me … I'm out of milk." Kathy handed me a few dollars and said, "When you get back I'll let you know what I need done." It was not a short walk to the store from her house, but I left without saying a word. The kids were busy playing in the yard, and I waved to them as I left.

The sense of dread that I had hoped would leave me after a good night's sleep, was stronger than ever. I felt as if an anvil sat on my head. Kathy and I were Catholics. Over the years, I had developed a daily habit of prayer and I took my Christian faith seriously. Kathy was less serious about religion. What no one knew about me, (something I never discussed with anyone in my family) was how much I had grown in my faith. I had grown to know the Lord Jesus and considered myself a Christian. The development of my faith began when I read the *Late Great Planet Earth*, a book by Hal Lindsey, published in 1970. I was fourteen. After reading that book, I better understood discernment and the many other gifts of God. I had always known things as a child. I can remember once, when I was only six or seven, trying to share with Mom something that I had "seen."

That particular morning I woke up early. I watched Mom get ready for work. In the room, I could see my mom's best friend, Margaret, standing next to her and looking at her. She was following Mom from room to room, but Mom was ignoring her. After a minute or two, Margaret began waving her arms wildly, trying to get Mom's attention. She seemed desperate to tell her something. "Mom," I asked her, "why are you ignoring Margaret. She wants to talk to you."

Mom grabbed me by my shoulders and shoved me against a wall. "Don't you ever— ever—say anything like that again! These are secrets to take to the grave. Do you understand me, Micky?"

I was wide-eyed and dumbfounded by Mom's reaction to my question.

I found out the next day that my Mom's best friend, Margaret, had died during the night.

After that, I learned to keep my mouth shut.

During the walk back from the grocery store, a sense of dread seemed to cover me in a cloud of doubt and fear for my sister. I was not sure where this foreboding came from, but I suspected it was connected to my sister's new boyfriend—Lee.

At the house, Kathy was busy in the kitchen cooking and the kids were still playing in the yard. "Thanks Mick, for picking up the milk for me." She said, as I walked into the back door. "I need the house to be spit-shined tonight and ready for Lee." Still feeling sick with dread, I started cleaning. It helped to get my mind off the horrible feeling of doom. It worked at first, but as the hour passed, the sense of evil grew stronger. I could not shrug it off. By eight that evening, I had finished cleaning the house. The kids had already come in from play, washed up, and had eaten an early dinner. After dinner, Kathy tucked them into bed.

Once the kids were down for the night, she busied herself with setting the breakfast-nook table with some of her best china and wine glasses. Admiring her handy-work, she looked at me and said, "Mick, when Lee gets here, I am going to introduce you and then I want you to go upstairs. Okay?"

"Okay. I'll say 'hello' and then make myself scarce." I had the good sense not to explore it further. By the tone of her voice, I knew it was not open for discussion or debate.

"He'll be here in about an hour." Her words struck me like a lightning bolt. It is coming ... the evil is coming ... into this house. These thoughts consumed my mind as I waited helplessly, knowing that my sister had invited this evil thing into her home. As the hours passed, my spirit became more restless and more alert. The hair on my forearms and back of my neck began to bristle.

I remembered the discussion I had with our next door neighbor at Mom's house a long time ago. My neighbor "dabbled," as she called it in the occult. She said that witches and warlocks could not just come into your home by themselves. "They have to be invited in," she had told me.

Kathy and I were standing together in the kitchen when we heard a motorcycle pull into the driveway. In that split-second, Kathy turned to me, she had a horrible look on her face. She grabbed me by my shoulder and said, "Just you remember ... HE IS MINE." I was stunned. She released my shoulders, and stared at me for a second.

Before I could react to Kathy's comment, George Lee Lutz opened the door. His long stride swayed across the living room floor. He embraced my sister and kissed her mouth. "Hello," he said. He gave Kathy what might pass for a smile, but something was wrong with that smile. My feet were immovable. My second sight and instinct were screaming at me. I actually ran my hand over the top of my head because it felt as though the hair on my head was standing on-end.

He was tall and thickly built. His blondish hair and blue eyes were striking against the black leather motorcycle jacket. He was wearing jeans and a polo shirt. His motorcycle helmet tucked under his arm, he stared at me and waited, his free arm wound possessively around my sister's tiny waist. "This is my kid sister, Mick," Kathy told him as she introduced me. He smiled at me, but it never reached his eyes.

"Well ... hello there," he said. I barely managed to mutter, "Hi." I did not extend my hand, as I would normally have done when greeting someone for the first time. I could not move. I felt a horrific sense of evil pressing in on me from all sides. My spirit was reeling.

I wanted to say my goodnights, and retreat to my bedroom when Lee said, "Don't run off just yet, little sister, have a glass of wine with us." I looked at Kathy. She nodded her approval and motioned for me to sit down at the table. Kathy poured wine into everyone's glass and sat down next to Lee. He did all of the talking, mostly on his favorite subject—himself. He went on and on, stopping every few minutes to kiss Kathy. She clung to his arm, her head leaning against his shoulder. I was not listening attentively—it all sounded like bragging to me. His skill in karate, and how he had once been a member of the motorcycle group, the "Hell's Angels." On and on.

I finished my glass of wine and said, "Goodnight." As I walked up the stairs, I realized that this man was a harbinger, a harbinger of terrible things to come. I was sure of it. From that moment on, there would be a division in my life and in Kathy's and her children's lives: *Before Lee,* and *After Lee.* I knew on a spiritual level that our lives would never be the same. Something wicked had entered our domain and it would not leave without extracting a price.

As exhausted as I felt, I struggled to fall asleep. One single reverberating thought kept repeating in my head:

Not who is he—but what is he?

The following day was Monday. Thankfully, Lee was gone. After the kids were off to school, Kathy drove me home. I did not know how to share with Kathy my dread and fear of her newfound boyfriend. Would she even hear what I had to say? I did not feel like talking, and I was relieved to be home. I wanted to be alone. I needed to think and to pray. My sister was in trouble. She was dealing with something she could never overcome. She was in danger, and so were the kids. But that danger did not come from this world … it came from another.

When Kathy picked me up from work, she told me she was not going to the diner that night for her regular shift. "I have something I have to do," she said. It all sounded mysterious but I did not ask her any questions. She seemed annoyed and preoccupied. Kathy's behavior was strange, even the kids asked me why Mom was acting so "weird." They never said much about Lee, but I had the feeling that they were afraid to say anything about him—to anyone.

Pulling into Kathy's driveway, the heaviness descended again. I wanted to escape. If it had not been for my niece and nephews, I would have stopped coming over. Nevertheless, I could not bring myself to leave the children alone with that man who had taken control of their mother.

In the corner of the kitchen, there was a huge new bag of dog food. I walked to the kitchen window, which faced the backyard. There was a large black dog tied to the swing set.

I spun around. "Kathy, you bought a dog … a full grown dog?"

She waved her hand in annoyance as she said, "That's Harry," she said, "he is Lee's dog … and now … well, now it's our dog. He is not the friendliest dog I have ever met, but hopefully he will fit in with time."

"What kind of dog is it? He's big."

"Lee says he is part Malamute and part Labrador." She did not seem happy about the dog but before she left to take care of her mysterious errand, she said, "Mick, can you feed and water the dog before the kids get home."

"Yeah, sure. I can do that."

I picked up the bag of dog food. It was nearly three in the afternoon. I had ten minutes to feed the dog before the kids got home.

The dog was sleeping on its side, the sun shining on his black fur. Two dog dishes were on the ground beside him and next to the back wall of the house. I rinsed out the water dish and refilled it with the garden hose.

When I turned around, the dog was awake and watching me. He did not move. No tail-wag, no upturned ears. He just watched. It was off-putting and strange. Most dogs are playful and excited with the prospect of fresh food and water on a hot day. But not Lee's dog.

That did not surprise me.

I squatted down, "Come on boy, don't you wanna eat? Come on."

The dog slowly got up and started towards me. He was not an old dog—maybe two or three years old at most. His weight was under sixty pounds, but he was pure muscle and yet, he seemed old beyond his years. He walked slowly as he came towards me. I wondered if Harry was in pain.

I felt sorry for him. He needed a bath. He got within two feet of me but refused to come closer, preferring to keep his distance even though I was laden with food and water.

I began to take to him gently. "What's the matter boy aren't you hungry?" Gradually he came closer, and allowed me to touch his head. I gave him a gentle pat and he began to eat. There were no tags on his worn, brown leather collar. As I picked up the bag of dog food and headed back into the house, I wondered if the dog was sick or traumatized. Kathy and the kids needed a puppy, not a full-grown dog. The kids were just getting to the door when I came back into the kitchen.

"Hi, Aunt Mick," they all shouted at once. "Can we have something to eat before we start on homework?"

"Sure," I told them.

Kathy's behavior continued to morph as the days and weeks of dating Lee droned on. She became sullen and withdrawn—more unreliable with each passing day. I was frightened for her and for the children. Something was taking hold of my sister. She was becoming someone I did not recognize. The woman I had known all my life was drifting away and I could do nothing to halt the process.

The next day I waited after work for Kathy to pick me up but she never came. I was worried. This was not like her to leave me at work with no ride and no message. Then again, my sister was not herself anymore.

I asked one of the other girls getting off work if she could give me a ride to Kathy's house. "No problem," she said. At Kathy's driveway, I gave her four dollars for gas money and thanked her for the ride.

My stomach was in knots. I did not feel good about any of this, but I had to find out if something bad had happened to my sister. Kathy's car was not in the drive way and the front door had been left unlocked. I opened the door with caution, not knowing what I might find.

"Kathy, are you in here?" I called as I walked through the front door. "Hey, kids, its Aunt Micky—are you home?" Still nothing. Complete silence.

Something's wrong, I thought to myself. It was past time for the kids to be home from school. I walked into the kitchen to see if they were having a snack. No one. I looked out the window into the backyard.

I gasped. It took a moment for my mind to register what I was seeing. Sick at my stomach, I ran out the back door, into the yard.

It was the swing set. It was one of those cheap, metal A-frames. Someone had removed the swings. Splayed upon the structure—the dog was in agony. Each leg tied with a rope, just past the shoulder and hip joints. The other end of the rope tied to the frame. His entire body suspended in the air—two feet off the ground.

What kind of human could do this to a poor dog? I was shaking with fear and outrage as I stepped closer to the suffering animal.

The poor creature moaned as I came nearer. He had trouble lifting his head, but he lifted his brows, to look at me. The look on his face broke my heart. It was a look of pain and shame. His eyes pleaded for help. Spittle and foam had accumulated along his lower jaw.

I ran as fast as I could into the kitchen and grabbed a sharp knife. As I struggled to cut through each rope, starting with his legs, the dog was still. There was no struggle. Perhaps he knew on some level that I was not there to hurt him.

Someone had tied several big knots in each piece of rope. When I had severed the final rope, he fell to the ground with a hard thump. His legs were stiff and he could barely move. I drug him to a shady spot in the yard, behind some bushes, along the back fence. The most painful part of the process was the dog's silence. I knew I was hurting him, but he never yelped, or struggled. It was as if he had given up on saving himself. He needed hydration, so I got his water bowl and sat it beside him.

I picked up all of the rope shavings and pieces and stuffed them into the outdoor garbage can. I had to remove all traces of this atrocity before Danny, Christopher, and Melissa got home. I could not allow them to witness such cruelty. My hands shook as I washed the knife and put it back into the drawer. They were red and sore from struggling with the rope and dragging the dog to safety. What kind of a person would do such a thing to an animal?

In my heart, I knew who was responsible for this—Lee. I was terrified that Kathy and the kids were in harm's way. I phoned Mom, without alarming her, I told her Kathy was not home, and I needed a ride. "Could you pick me up right away, Mom? I'm not feeling all that well."

She said she would be there in a few minutes. I locked the front door as I left but I knew that what we had to fear was not on the outside of that house, it was on the inside—invited in.

When we were riding home Mom asked, "Are you alright?"

"Yes, I'm fine. It was a rough day at work today, that's all." I told her it had been a long day and that I was tired and hungry. I did not want to scare her. I was scared enough for both of us.

That night after I went to bed, I wondered why anyone would do such a thing. It must have taken someone with great strength to do that. I was so exhausted. It did not take long to fall asleep. I dreamed about a demon that night; I could hear the sounds of a dog crying in my dream. I knew who had done this evil thing.

As the weeks rolled on, Lee began spending a lot more time with my sister—often spending the night. Although this was no surprise to me, I wondered if my sister really knew and understood this man. He had weaved a spell over her. She was no longer able to make wise decisions.

Incredibly, no one ever questioned me about the dog. Nothing. It was as if it had never happened. This, I was soon to discover, would become a familiar pattern. As things descended into madness, the silence grew deeper. It was as if Kathy could not see how strange their lives had become.

CHAPTER FOUR

through a glass, darkly

When I was not at Kathy's babysitting, I was there to help her clean house. Kathy had called that morning and asked if I could come over and "run the vacuum" because she had "something to take care of." She was adamant that I vacuum all the rooms.

Kathy seemed troubled and hurried as she left. I knew very little of what my sister's activities were these days. I had the sense that she was involved in something sinister, something bad, but she would never elaborate.

As I cleaned my way towards the upstairs, I thought about all of the bizarre changes that had taken place since Lee has arrived on the scene. Kathy had changed in every way. She dressed differently, spoke differently, acted differently ... she was a different person. The house had also changed. As my sister and her children grew more withdrawn, and darker, so did the house. The wall décor changed from pictures of green pastures and nature scenes, to pictures from the middle ages. Dark dioramas of mysterious creatures. The atmosphere was sullied. His personality dominated the space as it pushed out the personalities, likes, and desires of my sister and her children.

Kathy's (and now Lee's) bedroom was at the top of the stairs. The bedroom door was open. This never happened. Lee was fanatically private. He would bristle at even the hint of prying. Because of his zeal for privacy, I was hesitant to do any snooping around, but I also was determined to find out what was happening to Kathy. I dragged the vacuum cleaner into my sister's bedroom. The closet doors were open and I could see Lee's clothing. I suspected that he had moved in. Somehow, the thought of him spending all day, every day in this house, around my niece and nephews horrified me.

Her large dresser was against the wall next to the closet. It was one of her favorite pieces of furniture. It was everything else in her room that startled and captivated me. Once again, I felt the trembling warning of "second-sight." As I scanned the room, my eyes rested on the dresser and the nightstand. Everywhere I looked, there were stacks of books on the occult: on the dresser, the nightstand, stacks on the floor, next to her reading chair. It was a virtual library of the occult.

Witchcraft, meditation, mind power—how-to books about spells and incantations. There were small planters filled with occult herbs. I recognized them from my Christian studies on the occult.

On the dresser was some sort of a cross, I knew it had absolutely nothing to do with God. I was careful not to touch it. Beside the strange cross lay two open books. One was a book about an area of Long Island that dated back to the times of slavery. It had horrible graphic drawings. Depictions of demons and people being tortured. Pictures of bloody torsos, twisted in pain with mouths in silent screams were on page after page. Beside this book was a black bound notebook, filled with newspaper clippings about how some person in Amityville, Long Island, had murdered his entire family. I picked up one of the many newspaper clippings and read about the murders:

> *On the night of November 13, 1974, Ronald DeFeo, Jr. took a high-powered rifle and systematically shot his parents, and all four of his siblings in cold blood. Ronald "Butch" DeFeo, Jr., was twenty-three-years -old the night he killed his family. He shot his parents and siblings while they slept. His sister Dawn DeFeo was eighteen, Allison was thirteen, Marc was twelve, and the youngest sibling, John Matthew, was only nine-years -old.*

It was Thanksgiving week, the murders had happened only twelve days before. I carefully placed the notebook exactly as I had found it. I might throw up, I thought. I ran from the room into the bathroom. I had seen something I should not have seen. My sixth sense told me that no matter how carefully I hid my discovery, it would eventually catch up with me.

Even though I was determined that Kathy or Lee never find out about what I had seen, somehow, I knew that day would come. If Lee found out, there would be a price to pay. Although I could not foresee it then, in the passing of time, I would rue the day I had wandered into that bedroom. There would be a price—the ultimate price, which nearly took my life. It was only by the grace of God that I would survive.

I rolled up the cord to the vacuum cleaner and headed downstairs, relieved to be away from that room, those horrible books, and the trappings of the occult.

Once downstairs, I sat in the living room trying to compose myself before the school bus dropped off the kids. The bus pulled up to the corner and the kids came running inside. I rose to greet them on shaky legs. As always, I was happy that they were safe, at least for another day. Or, were they?

Danny was the first one inside the door. When I looked into this face, I knew something was wrong. As a child, he had not learned to hide his feelings like an adult. Everything he was feeling was visible on his face. He had been that way since he was a baby. All three of the children gave me big hugs, and then, without a word, they marched up stairs to put away their school bags.

After several minutes, they came back downstairs. Danny turned on the television and sat down on the couch. Although they had all given me a hug, not one of the children had uttered a sound since they had walked in the door. This was not normal. I had never seen them act this way—like little robots. I sat down between the two boys, but they did not move. I put my arms around Chris and drew him close in a hug.

"Are you alright, Chris?" I asked. He looked up at me and my heart broke. His eyes were welling up with tears. He squeezed me so tight it took my breath.

"Chris, what's wrong? You seem frightened. What is going on here?" Before he could share with me what had frightened him, Kathy's car pulled into the driveway. Chris's body stiffened as if preparing for a blow. Danny and Melissa sat frozen on the couch—waiting. When Kathy came in the door, she barely said hello before ordering the children outside, into the backseat of her car as she waited for me to get in beside her.

She dropped me off at Mom's house and said "goodbye," but the kids remained silent. As she backed the car out of the driveway, I turned to look back. They seemed so sad, but, there was something else … something heavy and evil weighed on those children. *He* held them captive. Not just their physical bodies, but also their minds, even their spirits—tangled in his evil web.

That night I cried myself to sleep and wrestled with the thought of trying to talk to Mom about the kids. They looked so unhappy. They were changing too. The children were becoming people I did not recognize. Kathy seemed oblivious to the problems her children were having and she was unable to listen to me, or to anyone else in her life … except of course, Lee.

It broke my heart to see them that way. I decided that it would be best not to say anything to Mom. She would worry and she too, would be unable to change Kathy's mind about Lee. If I had no power to change things, I could at least keep my eyes and ears open and my mouth shut. Learn what I could about the evil presence that had taken over my sister and her children.

When I look back on those days, I wonder if I made the right decision. Would it have been possible to stop my sister from entering into a lasting and legally binding relationship with this man? We cannot take back our steps in time, but some days, when I look back on what has happened I wonder: Could anyone have stopped what would happen next?

encounters

Two months later, Kathy called to ask if she could pick me up at the house. She and Lee were "going out" and she needed someone to watch the kids. Kathy seemed excited about where they were going, but she refused to say anything specific.

When Kathy and I walked through the back door, Lee was in the kitchen making a pot of coffee. The kids were in the living room watching television.

"I've already made dinner for the kids, Micky. It's on the stove," she said as she started up the steps. She hollered back to anyone who was listening, "I'm going to get dressed. I'll be back down in a minute."

Wanting to avoid being in the same room with Lee, I left the kitchen and went to sit with the kids on the couch. Lee placed three plates of food on the kitchen table. As if by unspoken command, all three children rose to their feet in perfect silence as they walked into the kitchen and sat down in front of their respective plates. Lee had already seated himself at the table. He stared at the children as they ate. Each child kept his or her head down, looking at their plate. They dared not look at him—this man who had hijacked their mother.

It was so odd. I could remember dinners at Kathy and Seb's house with the kids. There was laughter and jokes flew across the table like paper sleeves blown from drinking straws. At this table, with him, there was no laughter or fun. I turned the television set back on. The silence at the dinner table was just too eerie for me.

Lee watched everyone. He watched me, he watched the children. He watched Kathy. He kept his eye on all of us. I am sure it was a control issue.

"Finish all of your food, Danny," I hear him yell. He issued his command from on high to this young boy who was overwhelmed by the evil that had invaded his life.

Once the children had cleaned their plates (they did not dare leave anything behind), Lee put their plates in the sink. As he was finishing, Kathy came down the stairs. She was wearing a beautiful blue dress and a smile that ran from ear to ear. She looked lovely with her blonde shag haircut, and painted, red lips. The dress was low-cut, with a long, flowing skirt that hit her at mid-calve. She polished the outfit with a pair of ice-blue high-heels. "You look great, Kathy," I told her. Lee wore a suit and tie.

Kathy whispered to me, "Don't drink the coffee Lee made, Mick ... okay? It's for us ... later."

"Okay." I wondered at the time why she would ask me not to drink the coffee. Most people do not save coffee for later, preferring it hot and fresh. Reheated coffee is bitter. I found it to be a strange request.

As they headed for the door Kathy said, "Mick, I'm not sure when we will get back, but I will drive you home ... even if it's late. Okay?"

"That's fine," I said. The kids were sitting quietly on the couch, listening, but trying not be noticed. I turned to them and said, "Hey, let's find something fun to watch and I'll see if I can find us something good to snack on!"

I got three big cheers of "Yeah, Aunt Mick!" Danny jumped up and began changing channels, while Missy grabbed me by the leg. I picked her up, spun her around, and kissed her. She threw her head back and laughed.

Chris grabbed me and said, "Me too!" I spun him around and kissed him. They were all laughing as they sat down. I went into the kitchen to find something to eat. There were no cookies, no sweet goods or snack foods of any kind. I assumed Kathy probably had not gone grocery shopping for the week.

Searching the cabinets for popcorn or something to make for the kids, I opened a cabinet door, only to find row after row of jars. Each sealed jar was full of some type of spice. Some were green, some black, and some red. The jars were not like the ones you see for canning. Not Ball lids or Mason jars. They looked like old-fashioned apothecary jars—like the kind your grandmother's doctor or pharmacists might have used. I could remember seeing jars like that in an old movie. The jars were unlabeled. I found that strange, too. Kathy was an excellent cook but I wondered how she could know one spice from the other without any labels. After moving some things around, tucked away in the back of the cabinet, was a small jar of popcorn. I stuck my head into the living room and said, "Hey, how about popcorn?" I heard three big cheers.

It only took a few minutes to make popcorn. I filled a large bowl and carried it into the living room.

I froze. I was completely unprepared for what I saw.

They were asleep—sound asleep! I set the bowl down and just stood there. How could this be? I was scared. Was something wrong? Are they sick? I walked over to check on Danny and tried to wake him. He was unresponsive. When I shook his shoulder, he simply turned over and continued sleeping. Next, I checked Missy and then Chris. They were breathing, but asleep.

This cannot be normal. I glanced at the clock in the kitchen, nine o'clock. Lee and Kathy had only been gone thirty minutes.

What should I do? I decided to carry them, one by one, upstairs and put them in their beds. I checked each of them carefully as I tucked them in. They were such great kids. I kissed them goodnight and double-checked their breathing.

After tucking in the kids, I went downstairs and sat on the couch for a long time. I was afraid for them, for Kathy—even for me. They were not acting at all like the playful, happy children that I had known. I thought about Lee sitting there watching them eat— insisting they eat "every bite." The jars in the pantry and the strange looking spices, with no labels … it was all adding up to something that I didn't want to think about. God help us all, I think that Lee may be drugging the children. What about Kathy? Was my sister being *systematically* drugged?

The thought swept over me like a tidal wave. Could it be? Was Lee drugging the kids? There was something terribly wrong here. Kathy was not concerned about what was happening in this house. Why? Was she under a spell?

I ran back upstairs to check on the kids again. All sleeping. My sister's closed bedroom door gave me a sense of relief. I never wanted to see any of the stuff I had seen in there again. I cringed at the thought. As I walked back down the stairs, I decided to check the kitchen. I went over to the sink where Lee had placed the dirty dishes. Each plate clean. No food remnants. I looked at each piece, including the silverware. I raised the plates to my nose to see if I could detect a chemical smell, but there was nothing.

The coffee! I remembered what Kathy had whispered to me about the coffee. I walked over to the coffee pot and looked at it. I opened the lid and smelled it. It stunk to high heaven. I do not know what was in that coffee pot, but it was not coffee.

It was time to take a second look at those apothecary jars in the cabinet. I opened the door. There was nothing to give me a clue of what might be in those jars. There was nothing out of the ordinary in the refrigerator. Eggs, milk, butter, and a large clear plastic bag of coffee grounds sat on the bottom shelf. I checked on the kids for a third time. All fine. As I sat with the uneaten bowl of popcorn in my hand, I realized how angry I was. Even though I was starving, I was determined to eat nothing in that house. I emptied the bowl into the trash, washed and dried the dishes, and put them away.

Just to stay busy, I wiped down the counters and stove, and then swept the kitchen floor. I wanted to make sure there was no evidence of popcorn making. I carried the kitchen trash outside and dumped it into the garbage can. I felt strangely relieved to have gotten rid of all the popcorn.

When I looked at the clock in the kitchen, I was surprised at how fast time had passed. I checked the kids one last time, then took a seat on the couch, to wait. I just wanted to go home. Several hours later, I heard a car in the driveway. I felt bad about leaving the kids in this strange and frightening environment.

The next day Kathy called and asked me to help her straighten up the house and to watch the kids again. She and Lee were having a special meeting at her house, tonight. As I hung up the phone I wondered what she meant by "special meeting".

Kathy was at Mom's house in no time at all. As we rode in the car, I kept wondering what type of meeting they were hosting. After a few minutes, my curiosity got the best of me. "Kathy, what did you mean by a meeting?"

She waved her hand, as she answered, "Oh, just guests ... never mind."

We got busy cleaning. Kathy said Lee would be back soon and that she needed to get dressed.

I heard the kitchen door open and Lee hollered, "Kathy, they'll be here in a few minutes." In my mind, red flags were going up everywhere. My discernment was flying. I could feel the evil coming. Who or what is coming to this house?

Kathy came downstairs. She was fully made-up and she had on a nice pair of jeans, with a white peasant blouse. It was not like her to wear blue jeans, but they looked nice and she seemed to be comfortable in them.

Lee walked over to her, gave her a quick kiss and an embrace. "Are you ready?" He asked.

"Yes ... oh, yes!" Kathy exclaimed.

Ready for what? I wondered.

We quickly setup the kitchen table buffet-style. Kathy had prepared all of the food, it looked good but I was afraid to eat anything. I did not trust food cooked in this house. As Kathy set the final dish on the buffet, she turned to me and said, "Mick, when the guests arrive, can you take the kids downstairs?"

"Sure," I replied. The house had a nice finished basement with a couch and chairs and a second television. I would be happy to be away from the party and the guests. I felt such a presence of evil that I was wrestling inside myself. I could hardly think.

As I was gathering the kids together to get them downstairs, I heard the front door bell ring. Lee was greeting people as they came in. One woman saw me standing in the kitchen and made a beeline towards me. She was mid-forties, and her face prematurely wrinkled. Dressed from head to toe in black, she looked like something out of a scary movie. "Who are you? Are you Kathy's sister?" Her green eyes lined in black. I did not want to look at them. Without waiting, she moved closer to me, leaned in, and said, "Do you believe in transcendental meditation."

"No ... I don't."

"What about the power of the mind," she asked.

"No, I don't believe in that." She looked at me as if I were crazy.

"Surely you believe in the feminist movement, right?"

"I am not a member of the feminist movement. I work, and I believe in equal pay, but beyond that, I haven't given it a lot of thought."

"Well ... what are you ... some free-floating spirit?"

"No," I said, "Not at all. I do not believe in any of that stuff. I'm a Christian." Her eyes widened and she glared at me for a second, then spun around and walked back to the living room to join the other guests. Kathy had seen and heard some of our exchange and was giving me a dirty look.

"Okay, Mick," Kathy said. I knew it was time to take the kids downstairs.

Missy was already falling asleep on her feet. Halfway down, I picked her up and carried her to the large chair where she fell asleep. The boys piled onto the couch. They were out in minutes.

They were all asleep—again. How can these children hope to have a normal life, being drugged at night? I was angry and grieved. I began to pray. All of a sudden, I heard singing—at least at first I thought it was singing. In a moment, I realized that it was not singing at all. There were no actual words. It was some sort of chant ... or incantation. I had read about these things, but I had never heard anything quite like it. I stepped up my prayer. I have always known that the Word of the Lord can chase away demons. The angels "harken to God's Word." I knew that I needed all the help I could get to keep the entities that inhabited this house at bay.

For many years now, I had worn a cross around my neck inscribed with these words: "Thy kingdom come." It was my prize possession. I started to recite my prayer, "Our Father who art in heaven ...." The chanting upstairs stopped.

I continued with my prayer. When I came to the words, "Thy Kingdom come." My cross flew from my neck and catapulted into the wall about six feet in front of me. At that same time, I heard a hideous laugh from upstairs. The hairs on the back of my neck were tingling ... I was in a battle, a battle that I had to win. Without flinching, I continued with my prayer. I walked across the room to retrieve my necklace. I was not going to give in to intimidation and fear. I continued with my prayers and added the 92nd Psalm, the prayer of protection: "For he has given his angels charge over thee, and they shall keep thee in all thy ways. They shall lift thee up with their hands, lest ye dash your foot against a stone."

After an hour passed, Kathy came downstairs and said "Mick, it's time to go." I was ready to leave. I had discovered that night, what I knew in my heart had been the truth: My sister's boyfriend, Mr. George Lee Lutz, was a WARLOCK.

The meeting that Kathy and George had hosted that night was a meeting of witches: a coven meeting. I had never witnessed such a meeting in my life, and did not want to repeat the experience.

The next morning, Mom told me that my brother, Jimmy was coming over and we would all be going to Kathy's house. I was sick inside. I dreaded going but did not know how to tell Mom that I had no interest in being around a warlock. Mom, or my brother for that matter, would never believe me. It would only upset and frighten Mom. I knew that I was the only Christian in the family. Kathy had abnegated her faith to please Lee. There was no one for me to turn too. I hung onto the Lord.

My brother arrived and we headed over to Kathy's house. The evening passed quickly. Kathy and Jimmy had a good visit. They did not see each other much these days, but then Kathy did not see anyone much any-more—not since Lee had come on the scene. The evening wore on into the night. Mom had a good time, and after midnight, she announced that since it was so late, we should all spend the night at Kathy's house.

Mom said "goodnight" and went upstairs to bed with the kids in their room. My brother said he was tired too, and needed some sleep. Kathy told him he could use her bedroom for the night and he went upstairs. I decided that I would sleep on the floor next to Mom and the kids in their room. I started up the stairs when Lee said, "Wait a minute, Micky. Come and sit … have a glass of wine with us."

Kathy sat at the breakfast nook. I took a seat across from her. Lee came over with two glasses of wine in his hands. He sat a glass in front of both of us. He was drinking beer. As he started talking, I stopped listening. I was not paying attention. As Lee droned on about some feat or fantastic thing that he had done (he always talked about himself), Kathy reached over and took a large drink from her glass. Within seconds, she was slumped over in the nook and nearly unconscious. Minutes later, she was out cold!

Lee reached over, scooped her up, and carried her to the couch. When his back was turned, I dumped my wine in the sink, which was right next to me. When he came back to the table, I was sitting with an empty glass in front of me. As he took his seat, he spread his arms wide across the table. It made his imposing six-foot frame appear even larger. I was sure he was trying to frighten me. "Now … Micky," he roared.

However, I was not intimidated. I pointed my finger at him, saying. "Now? —Now nothing. I want to know exactly what you are getting my sister into! What are you doing to her ... and to my niece and nephews?"

Rage swept across his face as he lunged across the table and screamed, "Just who's avenging angel are you— Micky?" His voice was loud and deep. This growling, scowling figure should have frightened me, but for some reason, which I did not understand at the time, I was not afraid.

I leaned back as far as I could to escape his grasp. I looked him dead in the eye and said, "I'm no one's 'avenging angel' ... I'm just me!"

He sat back down. His fists were clinched, and the veins in his face pulsed. My brother, Jimmy was asleep in a bedroom at the top of the stairs. I was surprised that he had not heard Lee shout so viciously at me. *Jimmy has not come down to see what is happening. Why?*

I watched Lee's face—I did not dare turn my gaze away from him. He had turned his attention away from me and was looking at the stairs that went to the second floor. The staircase was to my right. He folded his arms across his chest and gave me a cold smile. He pointed toward the stairs and said, "Look, Micky. It's your brother." Then he laughed a maniacal laugh. The sound of it was like ice breaking under your feet.

As I looked in the direction of the stairs, I saw my brother. At least it looked like my brother, floating down the stairs. It took me a second to realize that his legs and feet were not moving. His feet were hovering about six inches above each tread as he moved methodically down the stairs. He was literally levitating down the stairs.

His face was expressionless. He was a zombie—like someone in a trance. It was as if his body was there, but not his mind.

When Jimmy reached the bottom of the stairs, he turned towards Lee and me. He began to speak, his face a frozen mask. It sounded like Jimmy's voice, and yet it seemed to come from somewhere else. It was almost as if there were two voices, but I could not be sure. Jimmy looked at us and shouted, "If you want a way to hell ... Mick ... we will get it for you." Then he turned and floated back up the stairs. There was no change of expression. Even though he called my name; it was like he did not know who I was. Surreal.

I looked back at Lee, his arms still crossed in front of his chest. His broad self-satisfied smile smeared across his face. He was beaming—proud of the monstrous spectacle he had somehow engineered. I wondered if this was some kind of cheap parlor trick or something far more sinister.

At that moment, I made my decision; to show fear to this man was suicide. I took a deep, slow breath, looked him in the eyes and smiled my biggest smile. I said, "Well, that was interesting."

He was livid. His circus-style antics had not frightened me, at least not that I had allowed him to see. Inside my heart was beating out of my chest, but outside I remained calm. Rage swept over him. He jumped up from the table, but this time he did not lunge at me. He strode across the living room, lifted Kathy from the couch like yesterday's dirty laundry and carried her downstairs, to the basement.

Once Lee took Kathy downstairs, I was alone for the first time all day. My hands were shaking. I felt somewhat proud of myself that I had not allowed him to frighten me. As I went over the day's events in my mind, I realized that he had drugged the wine. Why else would Kathy have passed out after taking only one swallow? After some time, I decided to lay on the couch in the living room rather than go upstairs. It was closer to the front door and I would be able to hear Lee if he walked up the stairs.

I thought about what had just happened. Had I really seen my brother float down the steps? My Irish sense of humor kicked in as I muttered under my breath, "So much for a backup plan." Had this entire evening been an exercise in intimidation? Why would Lee want to frighten me? Was he as afraid of me as I was afraid of him? As I drifted off to sleep I whispered, "I can do all things in the name of the Lord, who is my strength." I certainly was not going to let Lee scare me—no matter what little trick he organized for my benefit.

I kept hanging on to the hope that Lee would not live here all the time. He still had his own house, and Kathy had not mentioned marriage, at least not yet. I just had to pray that she never would.

***

A few days later Kathy said she needed some help moving boxes from Lee's house to hers. She picked me up at Mom's and off we went. I had never been to Lee's house and was not looking forward to going there. However, I did not want Kathy in that man's house alone. I decided to ignore my best instincts and go with my sister to his house.

The first thing I noticed was a wreath that hung on the front door. Kathy saw me looking at it. She explained to me that Lee had hung it there to remind "them" to have "Christmas all year long." I found the wreath odd and ugly. It did not look like any Christmas wreath I had ever seen. It was more like a funeral wreath: very dark green, with some strange black-colored berries nestled into the dark leaves. The ribbon, placed at the bottom of the wreath, was a black-green background with blood-red streaks running through it. It reminded me of real blood and veins. This was not your average Christmas wreath.

Inside, the house was empty. Against one wall, there were some boxes, sealed with tape and stuffed full. Kathy was bubbly. I realized that she was rambling on about her wedding plans. Oh, my God, surely she is not going to marry this creep. That is when she mentioned Lee's first wife. I stopped and looked into her eyes.

"What 'first wife?'" I asked. I could not believe that she had never mentioned this before. "Are you sure they are divorced?" Kathy laughed.

"Yes, silly, they are divorced, but even if they weren't it wouldn't matter … she disappeared. His first wife just vanished."

I stopped and looked at her.

"Kathy ... What do you mean ... she 'just vanished?'"

She waved her hands. "Just that ... she disappeared."

"How, Kathy ... how did she disappear. How does a grown woman vanish?"

"I don't know. Lee said she disappeared. I do not question him, Mick. That is not something that he likes, so I never do it. If Lee said she disappeared, than that is what happened." After that, she pretended to be busy moving boxes around, but I could tell she was avoiding the subject. I was seeing signs everywhere that this guy was not what he pretended to be. However, Kathy was blind to it. That blindness would get her into trouble one day. I hoped I was wrong, but a sense of foreboding hung around me. It has been there since Kathy first mentioned George Lee Lutz ... and now he was moving-in—permanently.

"Let's just get this done, shall we?" Kathy said. Not knowing what else to say, I got busy helping her move the boxes from the front room into the car. Once we were back at Kathy's, we moved the boxes from the car to inside. When we were finished, Kathy dropped me off at home.

At home, all I could think about was Lee's first wife. How had she disappeared? When? Under what circumstances? I longed to know the answers, but Lee kept his past well hidden, along with the rest of his secrets. Locked away where no one could get to them. God help me, I wondered if his first wife was even alive. What if he had done something to her, and now he was setting his sights on my sister. I felt powerless to stop her. No matter what I said or did, Kathy and Lee were soon to be married.

CHAPTER SIX

28 days and after

ocean drive

Kathy called. She needed my help moving some things. She told me the family (Kathy, Lee, and the kids) were moving into a house in Amityville. Lee had found the house, a rambling Dutch Colonial with some land that set next to a body of water. I knew the kids would love being on the water.

As we pulled into the driveway, I realized why she was so excited. "You won't believe what a deal we got on this house. We got it way under market value. Lee made a good deal."

"Why were you able to buy it so cheap, Kathy?" I asked her.

"I think something had happened in the house that wasn't good ... but we don't have to talk about that now." It was a big house—nestled next to the water, it was stately and sophisticated. The house looked familiar to me.

When I stepped inside, I felt that now-familiar feeling ... foreboding. The "knowing" that Mom had always cautioned me about as a child was ringing in my ears. This is not a good house. Lee will be very bad in this house. He will do bad things. It marks the beginning of many more sorrows for Kathy and her children.

As plainly as I heard the voice speaking into my spirit, I knew that the words he gave me were true. It was a prophetic warning. Something dark and dangerous is coming upon my sister's family.

The house had its own boat dock, complete with cover, in the back yard. Kathy was so excited. She loved the space and openness and could not wait for the children to experience living on the water.

We pulled a few more boxes from the car and went inside. It was enormous. She gave me a quick tour of all the downstairs rooms. It had five bedrooms and three baths, plus a half-bath. The kitchen was light and sunny with lots of room to cook. Kathy loved the big kitchen.

The main feature was a long peninsula counter-top. Kathy had lined up four stools along the counter.

Next, we ventured upstairs to see the expansive bedrooms. The large staircase was a work of art. The painted banister was thick and substantial. The wood painted with several coats of paint, but it felt cool to the skin as I laid my hand upon the banister.

Each room had large windows. The north side of the house faced the water. The south side had lovely views of the street and expansive side yard. The "Amityville House" as the kids called it was on 112 Ocean Avenue in the hamlet of Amityville. It was nothing like Kathy and Seb's old house where she and Lee had lived since they married. Although it was only a few miles away from her former house, it was oceans away in terms of status, neighborhood, and living comfort. It represented beauty and luxury that my sister had never known.

She glanced at her watch and said, "Oh God, we don't' have much time. We need to unpack as much as possible before we go." As we unpacked the car, she told me that Lee was very excited to be moving in. He had told her that it was going to make a "big difference in their lives." She mentioned again what a great deal Lee had found, how the property had been "blighted or something." I do not think Kathy knew what that term meant. She did not act as if she knew the history of the house.

"Mick, I think something happened in this house … before we moved here. But … I don't know what it was. Something not so good, but it gave us a chance to get a

good deal. I just love this house. Isn't it beautiful, Mick?"
When we were finished with the tour and the unpacking,
she drove me back home.

Once I was alone with my own thoughts, I knew I
must remember where I had seen a picture of that house.
As I sat in the reading chair beside my bed, I recalled the
day I had wandered into Kathy's bedroom. The day I saw
the books on the occult, and the history of witchcraft.
That was it. It came to me as suddenly as a bolt of lightning. That had been the house ... the house in the newspaper clippings. Something about a family killed ... in
that house ... the "Amityville house." A chill of knowing
ran across my body. This was Lee's doing. A blighted
property—people murdered ... an entire family had been
shot in their sleep—and now my sister and my niece and
nephews were living in that house.

As I sat in the chair, I closed my eyes and pictured
the house. An image flashed across my mind. It was Lee.
I could see his face as clear as if he were standing in front
of me. Once again, that word moved across my mind's
eye: W A R L O C K. There it was. Lee's face, then the
letters that formed the word. I understood. Lee was a
practicing warlock and he had my family! I grabbed the
dictionary in the bookcase in my bedroom:

> *Warlock, n. – a traitor; deceiver; liar]* 1. *A per-*
> *son perceived to have supernatural powers and*
> *knowledge by a supposed pact with evil spirits; a*
> *wizard; a sorcerer.* 2. *A traitor; a faithless per-*

son. 3. A dragon; a monster. 4. Conjurer or the like.

I tried to put the thought out of my mind. However, the dictionary had described my brother-in-law perfectly. I knew in my spirit what he was. I had known for quite some time now. I wondered how the kids were doing. Was he going to harm them? Had he already? How would Kathy defend herself against such evil?

Kathy, Lee and the kids had finally settled in at the Ocean Drive house in Amityville. She invited Mom and me to dinner in her new home. The unpacking was nearly complete, and Kathy wanted to show off her new house.

She led us into the living room. After some small talk, we decided to move to the kitchen so Kathy could put the last touches on dinner while she talked with Mom and me. After about twenty minutes, I heard Lee's car pull into the driveway. He came in the front door, but stayed in the living room.

"Mom, let me take you around for the grand tour, now that we have all the boxes unpacked. We'll go upstairs and check on the kids, too."

"Okay, Kathy, that sounds like fun," Mom said as she followed Kathy into the main hall and up the stairs.

Lee was sitting in the living room. I remained in the kitchen where I could stay out of his reach and attention. Knowing what he was capable of, being around him was more destabilizing than ever. Being in the same room with him filled me with dread. It was not fear, more like a loathing anticipation of having to thwart his manipulations. I felt relieved when it was time to go home.

***

Kathy called me and I could barely understand what she was saying. She sounded frightened. I heard Lee yelling in the background "What ... are ... you ... doing?" He screamed at my sister.

"Nothing, Lee ... nothing."

"Then hang up the damn phone ... NOW."

"Kathy—, Kathy ... are you still there? What's going on?" I asked. I felt frightened.

"Yes, I'm still here. I'm scared Mick, it's this house and L ....—."

"I ... SAID ... hang ... up ... THE DAMN ... PHONE," Lee shrieked in the background. The next thing I heard was the click of a disconnection. Kathy was gone.

I tried to call her back. She did not answer. I was sure Lee had forbidden her to take my call. I talked to Mom about it and she said they may be having a spat and that I should "stay out of it and let them work it out." It did not feel right. None of it felt right.

A few days later, Mom and I sat in the kitchen over a cup of coffee. She told me that she had spoken to Kathy earlier that day on the phone. Kathy had told her that they were "having problems in the new house. They are all frightened and need to leave the house right away."

"What's going on, Mom?" I asked her.

"Kathy asked me if she and Lee and the kids could come over and stay. I told her 'of course you can come … all of you can come.'"

(I decided that the best thing I could do was to keep my mouth shut. Apparently, Kathy was not saying much either.)

"Micky," Mom told me, "you'll have to move out of your bedroom and into the basement so we have room for Kathy and the kids."

"Pack up your room and move your things to the basement. You will be down there for a while."

I moved my things into the basement that night. Kathy and the kids moved in later that same night. To my great regret, so did Lee. The next day, Mom called me into her bedroom. "Promise me something, Micky. At no time will you ever be alone with Lee in this house. Do you promise? At NO time. Is that clear?"

"Yes Mom, I understand." She did not need to explain why I should never be alone in the house with Lee; I already knew what kind of a man we were all dealing with. Although Mom had little knowledge of spiritual things, she instinctively did not like or trust Lee.

That day I bought a jar of peanut butter, a small jar of jam, and a loaf of bread to keep in my new "basement bedroom." I had seen what Lee could do by tampering with food. I was determined to refuse him the opportunity to put any of his evil concoctions in my food. I was not going to eat anything in the house while he was there.

On Monday, Lee spent all morning on the phone. One call after another. As I passed through the living room, I overheard his conversation. He was talking with several newspaper reporters sharing his "story." Lee always had an angle. I could not help but believe that his sudden move from Amityville may have been part of a bigger plan. After he hung up the phone, Lee left the house telling Kathy he would be back "in a while."

This was my chance to speak with my sister without his presence. Kathy was sitting at the kitchen table, which was next to the wall phone. I sat down next to her and gently touched her hand. "Kathy, what is going on?" She grasped my hand tightly. I could feel her trembling as she began to tell me about things that had happened to them in the Amityville house.

"Mick, I knew the house was "blighted." The real estate agent told us that. Lee said it was not important and it was 'no big deal.' He said I was 'silly to worry about something that had happened so long ago.' Mick, you have to believe me—I never knew a family was murdered in that house. Had I known, I would never have consented to move into that place. You have to believe me, Mick. Lee never told me what had happened there or I would never have moved into that place."

She looked awful and she sounded sincere ... but my mind kept flashing back to the notebook in the bedroom that day. I chose to say nothing, and instead, just listened. She began to tell me the about the horrors of the Amityville house.

"Mick, it seemed like it started as soon as we moved in. I had a bad feeling that very first night. I called a priest to come and bless the house, but even the priest had some scary moments in the house. The kids were having nightmares. Windows were opening by themselves.

"One night I was getting ready for bed," my sister told me. "I was washing my face when I looked in the mirror, I saw this old woman looking back at me. Mick, I did not recognize her ... and yet ... I knew it had to be me! You remember when Jimmy and his wife came over to visit. The house was full of flies. They were everywhere, flying around the room, accumulating in the windowsills, and landing all over the kitchen counters. They were hanging onto the curtains—it was disgusting. Then Jimmy's wife Carrie thought she saw a child standing at the top of the stairs. It was scary. It got so bad toward the end, Mick, that we just could not stay another night. We really had no place else to go. That's how we ended up here ... back in West Babylon, with you and Mom."

I watched my sister's face as she related her story to me. She seemed genuinely frightened ... but still ... something was not right. She continued, "Lee is convinced that we were being "haunted" by the family that had been murdered in that house. I do not know if he is right about that or not, but I know that the Amityville house is the scariest, most bizarre place I have ever lived. I never want to go back there again."

"Kathy," I asked, "do you know what Lee plans to do next? Has he been talking to people, reporters, about what happened during your stay at the house?"

"I don't know, Mick. Lee doesn't say a lot about what he does, or who he talks too."

Kathy finished her stories fell silent. As if, she had finally relaxed for the first time in a long time. As we sat together, we heard someone open the front door. Kathy jumped up as if she had been electrically shocked. She placed her finger across her lips and gave me the shush-sign. Lee was back home. Instantly, Kathy's demeanor changed from relaxed to tense and agitated. She was in full-blown flight-or-fight response. Lee's presence in the house changed the atmosphere for all of us, but especially for my sister.

I remained seated at the table while Kathy fussed with the dirty dishes in the sink. Lee seemed annoyed when he came into the kitchen. He marched over to Kathy and grabbed her by her upper arm.

"I need to talk to you—right now!" He pulled her towards the bedroom. I heard the door slam. Powerless to help, I went downstairs to my room. Even from the basement, I could hear him shouting at Kathy. I could not make out what he was saying. I listened as closely as I could. I would not intervene in their business, unless he hit her. At that moment, it all seemed to come together for me—how frightened and frail Kathy had become. How the children had gone silent. They did not go out to play or even talk among themselves. They were like little automatons—programmed to speak only when someone spoke to them.

I thought about the phone conversations I had overheard between Lee and someone who was interested in hearing his story: "They were just innocent Christian victims," he told the person on the phone. "I knew something had happened in the house, but I never bothered to get the whole story. I was just happy to have the house at a great price."

He had lied about not knowing about the murders that had taken place in the Amityville house in November of '74. Only I knew that he had been researching the Amityville house since the day of the murders. I thought about the day Kathy took me with her to move some boxes into that house. How she had told me that Lee was "the one who found the house." How excited she was that day. I knew he had some "powers." He had demonstrated those powers the night I questioned him. Why would he pick that house? Lee came from a wealthy family. He could have picked any house he wanted. So why that one?

My head was spinning. How hard would it be for him to terrorize a woman and three little kids? I knew damned well that he was drugging them. I had experienced enough in my life that I believed in demons. I certainly believed in demonic activity. I did not believe in ghosts. Why would he go to the newspapers and tell them that they were being haunted?

I had the night off work, but preferred work to home these days. I did not want to be home hear him shouting at my sister. I did not want to mull over the evil circumstances that were overtaking my sister and her children. Maybe it was already too late.

I did not dare go upstairs to watch TV. Not with him sitting up there. He had put Harry, that pitiful, ugly dog in our backyard, which meant going outside was not an option. The way that dog acted, I wondered if he was drugging the dog too. I decided to read a book to take my mind away from the reality that was becoming increasingly threatening. I had been reading for quite a while when I heard someone calling me. It was Lee.

I called upstairs, "Yeah?"

"Micky, could you please come up here ... I would like to talk to you." I did not want to talk to Lee—not now or ever. The last thing I wanted was for him to come into the basement. I slowly walked up the stairs. A pot of coffee was brewing on the stove. As I entered the living room, Lee said, "Sit down, Micky."

He sat on the couch. He was wearing a blue-denim shirt, and jeans. Kathy sat next to him—she looked beaten down, defeated, but she said nothing. This man was a menace. Pure evil. I sat in the chair facing him. Kathy looked like a broken rag doll. Her body slumped slightly forward. She never looked up, not even when I sat down in front of her. She stared blankly at the floor. Her arms and hands were limp at her sides. What in God's name, has he given her? She is like a zombie. Lee smiled at me and began talking. "You know I've been thinking a lot about you, Micky. I think that I can help you—a lot."

"And exactly how are you going to help me, Lee?"

"Well, I can teach you about meditation, which I think you need. How to use the power of your mind and especially how to use the light within you."

I said nothing. I simply looked at him. Each time he paused, he would stare into my eyes. When his eyes met mine, I got a sinking sensation. It was as though he was trying to read my mind. As he stared, he kept droning on in a monotone cadence. I kept a furtive eye on Kathy as Lee continued to weave his spell. She never looked up or moved. It seems everyone who came under this man's control became a living zombie.

I stopped listening to his words, but I could feel the rhythm in the words ... "meditation is good for you ... you can connect with the light ... it is a calming influence...." His words flowed into my consciousness. This is how he does it, I thought to myself. This is how he controls them—hypnosis. I will not become one of his victims. I began to nod my head, but inwardly I was becoming more and more alert. At last, he finished by saying, "Now Micky, I want you to consider carefully what I am offering to teach you. Think about it and you can let me know." His eyes were empty.

I nodded my head and left the room. As I headed downstairs. I covered my mouth with my hand so Lee would not hear me laugh. Although I had beaten him at his own game, it was a hollow victory. Kathy had not been able to withstand his influence.

Intimidation had not worked on me, so now he was trying to recruit me. As far as I was concerned, he could keep his darkness, his witchcraft, his powers, and especially his "inner-light show."

There was no way he was going to move me from my faith.

CHAPTER SEVEN

cauldrons and

coffee pots

When I woke up, the sun was out and the house was quiet. I assumed everyone was still in bed. I went upstairs to use the bathroom. As I walked into the kitchen, I noticed a pot of coffee on the stove. I put my hand against it. It was still warm. I was so thirsty I decided I would have some.

I poured a cup and added milk and sugar—took a big sip and headed down the stairs. The next thing I remember, when I opened my eyes, I was on my back lying across the stairs. The coffee cup was still in my hand. The stairs all around me bore coffee stains. It must have spilled when I passed out. I had only made it halfway down the steps. *Is the coffee drugged?* I continued down the steps and into my room, where I sat and stared at the now-empty coffee cup. I looked at the clock; over two hours had elapsed. It did not take a genius to realize that whatever was in that coffee had knocked me off my feet and sent me into an unconscious oblivion. I have to talk to someone. This man may kill us all before it is over.

I ran upstairs and looked out the front door. Both Mom and Lee's cars were gone. I did not have much time. I was breathing fast. My heart was pounding. I ran back downstairs and threw on some jeans and a shirt. Dressed and ready to seek help for my family, I walked a few doors down to my friend Marilyn's house. Marilyn had known me since the day I was born. She knew my mom and had seen all of us kids grow up. I could trust her and I needed desperately to talk to someone. Her car was in the driveway, which usually meant she was home.

I took the three short steps to the front porch of her depression-era house. I knocked on the front door praying that she would answer. An overwhelming sense of relief washed over me as Marilyn opened her front door. "My God, Micky, you are as pale as a ghost. Are you alright?" Her eyes told me she was truly concerned for my well-being.

"Can I please come in Marilyn? I need to talk to you?"

She swung the screen door wide, and gestured me in. "Let's go upstairs to my room." I followed her upstairs. Marilyn was already dressed in black slacks and a light sweater. Her ample body easily navigated the steps even though she was in her fifties. She took a seat in her large reading chair while I sat on the edge of her bed. Behind the chair was a large ornate wooden bookcase with six shelves. It nearly touched the ceiling. Each shelf lined with hardback books. I had seen the bookcase many times and I was familiar with many of the books Marilyn read. Books on witchcraft and the occult filled one shelf. Although Marilyn was a devout Catholic, she was interested in exorcism and the occult.

"I know what I am going to say will sound crazy Marilyn, but please … hear me out. I think that Lee … my sister's husband, is a warlock."

She said nothing at first, but leaned back in her chair and looked at me for a long time before she spoke. When she did speak, the words echoed like thunder through my brain. "That's because you're right, Micky, Lee is a warlock. I have been watching him. I have seen him come and go and I can feel the power of his evil. Tell me, what has happened to have you so upset?"

I was so relieved I began to cry. Through my choked sobs, I told her some of the things that had happened. The yelling, the children acting like robots, the poisonous coffee, the strange jars of unmarked herbs … the screaming at my sister, her limp, non-responsive countenance after Lee was finished with her.. "He is drugging Kathy and the kids … I'm sure of it. I did not want to acknowledge it for a long time, but now, I believe he has drugged me. Now I know what he is doing."

I told her about the night I had questioned him and asked him exactly "what he was getting my sister into." I told her about his attempt to hypnotize me. "He talked to me last night ... told me he wants to ... 'teach me things.'" My hands were shaking. I began pacing back and forth in the large room. "He said he would teach me to use my 'inner-light.'" I told her about the terrible shouting that I overheard, about him grabbing my sister by the arm and dragging her into the bedroom.

"Micky, you have to understand how it works. When a warlock has control over his female, she ... Kathy ... belongs to him. She is his possession. Tell me Micky ... what is going on with that dog in your backyard? Is that Lee's dog?"

"It's his, but ... that dog is weird. His name is Harry, but he does not respond to his name, at least not to me or to anyone ... except Lee. He acts like a very old dog, but I do not think he is that old. I believe that Lee is drugging the dog along with his wife and stepchildren ... and now ... me." I shared with Marilyn how I had found the dog tied to a swing-set one day at Kathy's old house before she and Lee were married. "Marilyn, I cut the dog down as soon as I found him. It was terrible. He was suffering so much. Yet, after I set him free, and tended to him, no one ever talked about the dog ... or about what happened to him. It was as if it never happened ... but it did. No one ever said a word."

"I want you to try and remember that night, when Kathy was still at her house and you had come over for dinner. You told me Lee had demonstrated his powers to you. Before he told you to 'look' … what were you thinking?"

I told her I was wondering how my brother could sleep upstairs without hearing Lee scream at me.

"Micky, listen to me very carefully," Marilyn said, "I think you are in great danger. The funny feeling you had when he stared into your eyes, the way he did tells you he can probably see your thoughts. You must be careful of your thoughts when he is around you. The fact that he has offered to "teach you things" tells me that he is beginning to see you as a threat. You must guard your thoughts. I want to show you something."

"Marilyn, I wanted to tell you that no one is ever allowed to touch Lee's coffee … not even Kathy. He is extremely guarded about it. Now we know why … it's one of his weapons."

Marilyn reached into her dresser drawer and pulled out a book. It was an old, tattered hardback, much smaller than the books you see today. The leather binding was faded and scratched. It looked to be decades old. It was a book about the occult and spell casting. She said she had bought it at a yard sale long ago. She thought the woman who sold it to her was a witch.

"It's all in this book, Micky. It tells you all about witches and warlocks. How to cast spells, how to control others, and how to put a curse on someone. It also talks about herbs, crystals, and jewelry that are important to people who practice witchcraft." She did not offer the book to me. She knew I would never take it.

"What does it say, Marilyn ... what can I do to be free of this man. What can I do to get my sister and her kids free?"

"I'm not sure how to help you," She said. "Do you think you can bring me some of that coffee?"

I told her there was a big bag of it in the refrigerator and that as long as no one was home when I went back to the house, I would take a coffee sample and bring it to her.

"Hurry and see if you can bring me back a sample," she said. I looked out the window. The driveway was still empty. I ran as fast as I could.

I was breathless when I walked into the kitchen. I grabbed a piece of aluminum foil from the cabinet, then took the bag of coffee grounds from the refrigerator and put a small amount into the foil. Not too much. I carefully put the coffee back exactly as it was. I was back at Marilyn's in just a couple of minutes.

"That's great Micky, thanks," Marilyn said as she took the small foil pouch from my hand. "Check back with me in a few days ... and remember Micky, guard your thoughts."

I ran back to the house and downstairs to my room. I felt so relieved to have actually spoken to someone. I thought about how she had warned me to "guard my thoughts." Marilyn believed that I was in great danger. I had to take this threat seriously. I said a prayer to the Lord, and decided that whenever Lee was around I would simply keep the words "Jesus is Lord" running repeatedly in my head. It was only a few minutes before I heard Lee, Kathy, and the kids coming in the front door.

During the next two days, I tried my best to avoid Lee whenever he was in the house. He was on some sort of a rampage—angry all the time, snapping at Kathy and the kids. Raging at small things. One afternoon I saw him grab Kathy by her arm and yank her out of her chair. She did not protest. He dragged her towards their bedroom. I had seen this scenario play out many times. Lee would get angry, grab Kathy and drag her into the bedroom. When Kathy came out of the bedroom, she would be a walking zombie. It grieved me. My only hope was that Marilyn would have some concrete proof that Lee was drugging the family—his evil was palpable.

I had always admired my sister. Kathy was pretty. She had been a spitfire before she married Lee. The kind of girl who was not going to take crap from anyone. That was how she was when she was married to Seb. Not now. I remembered Marilyn's words: "she is his possession." Deep in my heart, I knew Marilyn's words were true. The sister I had known no longer existed. All that remained was the shell of the person Kathy had been.

I kept the words "Jesus is Lord" in my head whenever I walked past Lee's room or whenever I was unlucky enough to be around him. I felt like I could peel his eyes from my back when he passed me in the hallway. I was sure he was wondering why I had not said anything about his offer.

It was Friday, two days after I had given the coffee sample to Marilyn. A newspaper reporter came by the house to speak with Lee. It was not hard to guess he was a reporter. The name of the newspaper was on the side of his car. Lee met the reporter outside, in the front yard while Kathy stayed inside. I supposed she was not "allowed" to take part in the meeting.

On Saturday morning, Mom left to pick up my Aunt Nellie at the train station. She was coming over to visit for the day. I loved my Aunt Nell. Getting a visit from Aunt Nell was better than having Santa Claus as a guest. She always brought candy and small gifts. When Aunt Nell came in the door, she greeted me with a big hug. I was so glad to see her. Mom got busy preparing lunch for us in the kitchen while Aunt Nell and I sat at the kitchen table getting caught-up and laughing. It all seemed so normal—so happy. "I brought you something, Micky." She reached into her purse and handed me a small box of Godiva chocolates. Even now at the age of nineteen, having Aunt Nell around was like a holiday.

I gave her a big hug. Mom had finished preparing lunch, so we all sat down together to eat. I felt safe and normal for the first time since Lee and Kathy had moved into Mom's house.

Just as I was starting to let my guard down, Lee burst into the room. He had Danny, Chris, and Missy standing in front of him. They were in a line like soldiers, side by side. Stiff and silent.

"Go and say 'hello,'" he barked to the children.

One by one, each of the kids came over to Aunt Nell and hugged her. After a hug, each child politely said "hello," then turned and left the room. Robots—sick, frightened little robots. That moment solidified my distrust and dislike of George Lee Lutz. For a split second, I looked at my mother. She returned my gaze. She had to know that this behavior by her grandchildren was not right. Not healthy, or normal. I was not sure Aunt Nell would notice how mechanical her great niece and nephews had become.

Lee banished the children to their room, then came back into the kitchen and sat down at the table. Mom stood up and said, "Mick can you clean this up?" I heard her go down the hallway and into her bedroom and close the door. Lee wasted no time. He began turning on the charm with Aunt Nell as I began clearing the table. I heard him offer to get her a cup of coffee. The hair on the back of my neck stood up. I tried to keep the words "Jesus is Lord" playing in my mind.

Damn him and that toxic, poisonous coffee. There was always a pot of his coffee at the ready, warm, hot and dangerous. He was the only one allowed to make it. He would bring Kathy a cup of it every morning. As I washed the dishes in the sink, I watched as closely as I could without drawing his attention. He heated some tap water. Filled the coffee cup to the halfway point with the hot coffee—then added warm tap water. Handing the steaming cup to Aunt Nell, he smiled and said, "Here you go Aunt Nell … enjoy." As Nell lifted the coffee to her mouth, I realized that the sip of coffee that I had taken

the other morning had been undiluted. I had gotten the
full dose, but Aunt Nell, gratefully was getting a more
diluted solution. As she drank her "coffee", I steamed
with anger. How can he have the nerve to drug my sister,
my niece and nephews, and now my aunt? He is a monster.

He chatted with Aunt Nell as though everything was
perfect and normal. She had downed about a third of the
coffee when Lee suggested they go into the living room
and watch TV. I stayed at the kitchen table, pretending to
read a magazine. I was worried. It did not take long for
Aunt Nell to fall asleep on the couch. She slept for about
an hour and a half when Mom came out and woke her up
so she could make the train on time. Lee had left as soon
as Aunt Nell had fallen asleep. I had not heard a peep out
of Kathy or the kids all afternoon. I hugged Aunt Nell
goodbye and she and Mom left for the train station. I
went back downstairs to my room.

Lee had destroyed what might have been a lovely afternoon. Obviously, he had not wanted any interaction
between the family and Aunt Nell. Best to keep the family secrets closely guarded. There was no better way to do
that than to drug everyone.

I had to find out what he was putting in that coffee.
Maybe Marilyn had figured it out and could tell me what
to do. "First thing tomorrow, I will see if she is home," I
said to myself. Sleep escaped me. My thoughts were rac-
ing and I was still seething with anger over Lee's treatment of my Aunt Nell.

I could hear Lee's heavy footsteps on the floor above. He had put the kids to bed, and then he walked across the living room, to where Kathy slept. I felt so sorry for her, and yet, I could see no way to wake her up from this nightmare.

The house settled down. I slowly drifted off to sleep.

CHAPTER EIGHT

holy water

It was Sunday morning and I decided to walk to the local market for a loaf of bread. As I walked, I thought about the day before and the visit from Aunt Nell. Aunt Nell never fell asleep when she came to visit. I kept recalling the look in my mother's eyes when Lee told the children to "say hello to Aunt Nell." They were like little machines, programmed by the puppeteer to perform as expected.

As I continued my walk, I noticed that Marilyn's car was not in her driveway. I was disappointed. I needed to talk to someone who understood my problem.

A moment later, a car behind me slowed down and came to a stop. I heard someone shout, "Hey, Micky." I turned around and recognized two friends from school.

"Hey, you guys, it's good to see you," I said smiling. It was Jenny and Erica from the neighborhood. We had all grown up together just a few blocks apart. They had been my schoolmates for as long as I could remember.

"Where are you going, can we give you a ride someplace, Mick?"

"Sure. I was going to Our Lady of Grace. That would be great if you can give me a lift."

"Hop in." I had originally intended to walk to the market but since I had a ride, the church sounded good to me.

The church was less than a mile from my house so it only took a few minutes before they dropped me off. I thanked them for the ride.

When I entered the church, I could tell the mass was almost over so I quietly sat in the back row. As I prayed to the Lord, I felt confused and frightened about everything going on at home. As the mass ended, people filed out. Some greeted one another and said their goodbyes until next Sunday. Others smiled at me on their way out of the sanctuary.

I decided to stay a few minutes longer to pray. I rose to leave and that is when I saw it: the Holy Water. There was a small marble bowl on a tall pedestal just to the side of the main door that lead to the narthex. Beside the holy water, there were several small glass vials. As a Catholic, I knew that I was free to take some of the blessed water with me in one of the small vials. I filled one and put it in the pocket of my jacket.

As I walked home, I passed the market and bought the loaf of bread that I needed. The walk home was a nice respite from the turmoil that I felt at home.

When I got back to the house, both cars were gone so I guessed I would have the house all to myself. The way I was feeling, so alone and desperate to make a change, it felt good to know he was not there. I was mistaken. When I opened the unlocked front door, the television set was on and the kids were sitting on the couch.

Kathy was in the kitchen washing dishes at the sink. "Hi Kath," I said as I walked over to her. "I brought you something." I pulled the vial out of my pocket and held it in my open palm.

She glanced at it and said, "What's that?"

"It's holy water." She stared at me. Her expression changed from wonder to anger. She snatched the vial from my still-open hand and flung the small bottle across the sink where it landed with a considerable "clank" against the windowsill.

"Micky, where did you get that … thing … and why in the hell did you bring it to me?" She stood stone faced, waiting for my answer.

"Kath, I got it from church. You know very well what it is. Don't tell me you have forgotten what holy water is … you were raised a Catholic—just like me."

She said nothing and continued to wash the dishes. I felt overwhelmed. I had to try to reach my sister. While I had her alone, before George Lee Lutz could completely take her over. Without premeditation, I reached across her hands and turned off the water.

"Kathy I want you to sit down here and listen to me." I pointed to a kitchen chair.

Kathy was looking at me with an expression of disbelief. God knows that I had never spoken to Kathy with that tone of voice. She was my older sister. I looked up to her, or I had. I would never have ordered her to do anything. However, this time things were different. I had to push past my fear and somehow reach her. I needed to reach the sister I had known all my life ... before she was gone forever. After a long pause, she sat down. I sat beside her and began to explain that although we were raised as Catholics, I had learned a great deal since we were kids.

I talked to her about Jesus. She listened without interruption, but there was an invisible wall between us. I knew the architect of that wall—Lee. It always came back to Lee.

She did not say anything as I spoke to her. Her head bowed, she stared at the floor. I had said what I wanted to say. I got up, took my loaf of bread, and walked downstairs. A few minutes later, I heard the water running in the sink. Had my words had any impact? There was no good way to tell. At least I had tried to reach her before it was too late. Kathy would be in more trouble if she decided to share our conversation with Lee. He would never approve of my talking to Kathy about her beliefs. After all, her beliefs were no longer up to her ... they were now under his control.

Thirty minutes later, I heard Lee come in the front door. The evil that was his constant companion began to fill the house with the atmosphere of dread. Every one scattered like rodents when he walked in the door.

How much longer would my sister endure the torture of her psyche and that of her children? When would she decide to get away from him? My intuition told me that time was running out for Kathy to save herself.

My only option was to control my fear, and by doing so, keep him from controlling me. I knew that no matter the cost, I was not going to show him any fear. Not anymore.

CHAPTER NINE

the hoax

Later that Sunday afternoon, I was anxiously watching for Marilyn' car. Every few minutes I would run upstairs to check again. A little after five, I saw her old Chevy pull into the driveway. Thank God, she is home. I ran out the front door and up the sidewalk to greet her.

"Marilyn, I'm so glad you are back. Did you find out anything … about … you know?"

"Come into the house a minute, Micky." We sat at her kitchen table as she pulled off her coat and put on some water for tea. "Have you been doing what I asked? To guard your thoughts?"

"You bet," I told her, "it has been hard, but every time he comes near me, I concentrate on a Bible passage or a quote, anything to keep my mind from attack."

She nodded her head. "Has he said anything more to you about teaching you, or meditating?"

"No, Marilyn, not one word. Thank God!"

"He's probably wondering what you are doing, Micky. As I told you, he may be starting to perceive you as a threat because you know what he is. You know what he is trying to do. At least part of it anyway."

"What did you find out ... about the coffee, I mean?"

"You know Micky, I have friends, and those friends know about the occult and occult practices. I have been talking to them a lot about your situation ... without mentioning your name, of course. I also have friends in the police department. I took the coffee sample you gave me to the New York state police and had it analyzed. Everything in that coffee is of an occult nature, there is a definite presence of a drug in it—but not enough to determine what the drug is."

"I know there was not much," I replied, "but I was afraid to take too much. I cannot afford to have Lee catch on to what we are doing. You must promise me, Marilyn, never to tell anyone who I am. You must help me keep my secret. I believe that lives may depend on it."

"No. No-no, Micky. I have not told a soul. I believe you are right. I do think someone could be hurt if Lutz found out what we are doing. I don't want you to be murdered and I don't want him coming after me."

"I've been thinking about it Marilyn, when he gave the coffee to Aunt Nell, it had been diluted. Remember how I told you he filled her cup to the halfway point. He added water to fill the cup to the top?"

"Yes, I remember that," Marilyn replied.

"Well, when I had poured some of the coffee into my cup a few days earlier, it had not been diluted. Because it was full-strength, I passed out cold on the stairs. It is a miracle I did not break my neck. I was out for over two hours."

"That's interesting. If you get a chance, try to bring me more, a larger sample this time. Do you think you can do that?"

"I'll try, but he is watching me all the time. It could be hard."

I gave her a brief hug and headed home. It was after six and almost time to go to work. I got ready and waited for the couple I car-pool with to pick me up. They lived near me and we all worked at the same factory.

That night at work, I thought about what Marilyn had told me. The state police. Marilyn had actually gotten the state police involved. I was frightened and relieved at the same time. Frightened at what Lee might be doing and relieved that I was right.

When I got off at two a.m., it was dark and cold. My friends dropped me off at the house and all was quiet. I assumed that everyone was still in bed. No lights were on. I was starving. I decided to open the refrigerator and see if I could find anything safe to eat. With Lee, you could not be too careful. There was an open package of Kraft cheese slices, the individually wrapped kind. That might be safe, I thought as I removed the package. I took one slice from the middle of the stack and began to look it over carefully. It looked okay.

Without warning, I heard pounding footsteps bounding across the kitchen floor. Lee had been sitting in the dark living room and now he was after me. He came stomping at me with his fists clenched at his sides. His breath was labored. Small droplets of sweat beaded his forehead. He screamed as he came at me, "What do you think you are doing?" He shouted. I could smell his breath; he was standing so close to me.

"That's my food." His rage was barely under control. He raised his white-knuckled fists as if he were going to hit me. He was in such a state that his cheeks were puffing in and out, as he breathed. He towered over me. Somehow, I had sense enough not to move. I chose to stand my ground, feeling that it was the best way to be safe.

I marshaled a calm that came from deep in my spirit. I looked him in the eye and said, "What are you going to do, Lee—hit me? Just—try—it—!"

He took a step backwards and looked at me for a few moments. Then, he seemed to deflate, like a soufflé jarred by a slamming oven door. He was not accustomed to being backed-down. Seeing others cower before him was what Lee lived for. It gave him energy. He gained strength from the fear of others. I was not about to give him any ammunition.

I opened the refrigerator door and threw the slice of cheese on the top shelf. It made a smacking noise against the cold glass. I slammed the door and walked past him without looking into his face. I went straight to the basement stairs. My ears listening for any sound that would indicate he was following me. I heard nothing.

When I got downstairs, I could hear him stomp across the living room and into his and Kathy's bedroom. Slam. The door made a shudder that must have awakened the entire house. I took off my coat and sat down. What in the hell just happened?

The strange part was I had not come into the house by the back door, but through the front door. The living room was empty. He was not in the living room when I came in and I never heard him come out of the bedroom either. Had he been hiding—waiting for me? Was he sneaking around watching me? In complete silence? He had to have been watching me all the time. How many nights, I wondered had he been watching?

I had dared him to do something, "just try it," I had told him. I felt proud of myself—I had not backed down. I was through being bullied—tired of tiptoeing around the warlock. I was tired of his evil; tired of watching him abuse Kathy and the kids. I was exhausted and found myself in an almost constant vigilant state. It was a nightmare. I could only imagine how tough it was for Kathy.

It did not take long to fall asleep.

I got through the next day by staying in my room and going to work at night. My boss had told us that we would all have Thursday night off because a shipment of materials was undelivered and probably would not arrive before Friday. The way things were going at the house, I was not looking forward to having an extra night at home. I stayed in the basement and read a book. When I heard Lee and Kathy in their bedroom arguing, I snuck upstairs and got a jar of peanut butter I had hidden, and took it back downstairs.

On Thursday morning, I woke up early listening to heavy banging upstairs. I had only been asleep a short time. The banging was coming from the living room. I could tell by the heavy footsteps that it was Lee. He was muttering loudly to himself and it sounded like he was moving furniture.

I got up, slipped on my coat and very quietly went out the back door. I went around the corner of the house and looked at the driveway. Both cars were gone. I quietly slipped back in the door and back down the stairs. Where did Kathy go? She never left the house anymore unless Lee was with her. Never. I remembered the promise I had made to Mom to "never be alone with Lee in the house."

I decided my best course of action was to be quiet. Lee would think I was sleeping. He was still moving furniture in the living room. He kept stopping, then stomping back and forth. First to the bedroom, then back to the living room. A few minutes later the cycle would repeat. This went on for over an hour. Bang, bang, bang. At last, the banging stopped and I heard him walk into the kitchen.

Again. Bang. Bang. Bang. What in God's name is he doing? He was moving the kitchen table and chairs. Why? After a few minutes he would walk back to the bedroom, then back to the kitchen and then to the living room.

After thirty minutes in the kitchen, I heard a strange noise coming from the side of the house. I had to know what was going on. I slowly crept up the stairs. No sign of Lee. I stepped silently to the back door and opened it.

The houses were very close together on that side. Only a few feet apart. When we were kids, we would go on that side of the house because if you yelled it would make echoes. I noticed that Lee had opened the bedroom window—it was wide open. I watched his hands stick what looked like a tape recorder in and out of the window. He kept turning it on and off. Each time he turned it on it played horrible sounds. Moaning and groaning sounds that sounded like someone dying or being desperately hurt. I was not sure what to make of it. He pulled the recorder back and began to close the window. That was my cue to slip back downstairs before he came out of the bedroom and discovered me upstairs.

Those sounds were "ghostly" noises. If you heard them in the night, you would swear it was a ghost or a spirit. What is he doing? Why does he have that tape recorder and why the awful sound effects? Why was he moving all the furniture? None of it made any sense.

As I listened from the basement, I heard the front door close. I ran upstairs to look out the front window. Kathy had pulled into the driveway. Lee got into the passenger side. Off they went. I stood in the living room and looked around. All of the furniture had been re-positioned just as it had been before the banging. I went into the kitchen; all of the furniture there was also in place. Why would he move all of the furniture and then put it back where it was?

That is when I saw it. The bedroom door had a new lock. A shiny new lock that looked much more substantial than the old one. That had been my bedroom and I knew I had never had a strong lock on the door. I had no need for a lock on my bedroom door ... but that was before Lee moved in.

I was still tired so I decided to try to get some sleep. In the afternoon, I called my boss at work. He said the night shift would be off until Monday night because the shipment had not arrived.

I decided to bundle-up and walk to the local market. It was brutally cold, but I needed to get out of the house. I took my time in the store and picked up a small package of coffee and a loaf of bread. On the way home, I picked up the pace. It was already past dusk and the wind was starting to blow harder. It chilled me to the bone. As I neared the house, I noticed a car I did not recognize parked out-front. Kathy's car was in the driveway, but Mom's car was gone.

As I walked to the front door, I stopped to read the license plate on the back of the strange car. It was a local plate. The letters on the plated spelled out the word "demon." As I approached the front of the car, I saw that the vanity plate also read "demon."

"What now," I muttered as I climbed the stairs that led to the front porch. As I brushed my feet off on the mat and stepped inside, I could hear Lee, talking about a "book" being written about "their story." He sounded excited. I knew they were not expecting me to be home.

As I stepped into the kitchen, Lee stopped talking. There was an older couple seated at the kitchen table. A man and a woman. Seated beside them at one end of the table sat a priest. Lee sat at the opposite end. Kathy sat across from the couple with her back to me.

The priest was slumped forward in his chair staring at the floor. I made a mental note of the half-empty cups of coffee in front of each of them. I could smell the funny odor of that coffee as soon as I had entered the kitchen. Lee mixed a batch of that witches' brew every day. He shot me a look that told me he was annoyed by my presence. Despite his annoyance, he said, "This is Kathy's sister, Micky."

The couple nodded and said, "Hello." I smiled and nodded.

"Micky," Lee said, "this is Mr. and Mrs. Warren ... and this is Father Ray," he said, gesturing toward the nearly comatose priest.

I stepped closer to the priest. "Hello, Father." I extended my hand to shake his but he did not respond. His body never moved, instead he seemed to be in trance-like state. Staring at the floor without any sign of cognition. After what seemed like an eternity, and with great mental effort on his part, he slowly raised his head and extended a shaky hand.

"How are you, Father?" I asked. He looked up for just a moment as if he were going to speak. Then he simply dropped his head, and began to stare at the floor again. My sister and the couple across the table were taking this all in. Kathy did not say anything and neither did the couple. I felt like I was in a horror show. It was terrible. All I wanted to do was to get away from these crazy people.

As I headed downstairs, I heard Lee resume talking. His was the only voice I heard. Lee always dominated every conversation.

I took off my scarf and coat and wrapped a blanket around me. I was cold. A few minutes later, I heard the chairs at the kitchen table pulled back and then footsteps going to the front door.

Apparently, the meeting was over. A few minutes later Kathy and Lee walked to their bedroom and shut the door. I heard the now familiar, "click" of the new deadbolt on the bedroom door. I thought about the strange license plate on the car and the way the priest had acted ... *now he is drugging a priest, too.*

The warmth of the blanket engulfed me and I soon fell asleep. Mom did not come home that night, but no one offered me any explanation.

Mom called in the morning and explained that Aunt Nellie had needed her and she was at her apartment. She said she would be home sometime on Sunday. As I hung up the phone, I wished that she had taken me with her. She did not know that I was off for the weekend.

I ran downstairs and grabbed the package of coffee that I had purchased at the store. Upstairs I took the old coffee pot from the cabinet, rinsed it out, and put a pot of real coffee on the stove.

Since I had the house all to myself, which almost never happened, I decided I would watch a little television. I happily selected an old movie. It felt great to just relax and enjoy a normal moment in my own house. I went into the kitchen and poured myself a cup of fresh coffee.

The hours flew by blissfully, but as all good things must end, so did my peaceful afternoon. I heard a car pull into the driveway. It was Kathy, Lee, and the kids. My afternoon was over. I switched off the television and headed downstairs when I remembered my fresh pot of coffee on the stove. I picked up the hot pot by the handle and carefully navigated my way back into my bedroom dungeon.

I was careful to put Lee's coffee pot where it had been when he left. Just as my foot hit the last stair, I heard the front door open. Lee was yelling at Kathy as they came in. "Why can't you do anything right, you are so stupid. I can't believe I married you," he yelled. The kids were silent. Then I heard, "Go to your rooms, you little brats. I don't want to hear a peep out of you … any of you." I heard the kids scatter like a startled flock of birds.

One by one, bedroom doors slammed shut. I could hear Lee's raised voice but could not understand what he was yelling. So much for this day. I had felt happy and relieved for a few hours, but I knew it could not last. After several minutes, the yelling stopped. Lee had his fill of vitriol for the day. It was quiet now. I read a book for a while and then fell asleep.

***

The day I met Aaron was a good day. I was putting out the trash in front of the house when a very fancy car drove up the block. I watched. The driver stopped the car and got out to speak to me. He was young and good looking and he asked me if I wanted to take in a movie. I could hardly get the word "yes" out of my mouth. I was completely overwhelmed. That was how it had started with Aaron O'Reilly and me. I was love-struck from the start. He was a rakish, handsome, Irish bad-boy who drove a great car, and had lots of cash. He made great money as a carpet-layer. In those days, the housing market was booming and there was work all over the country for journeyman carpet-layers. Aaron was ten years older. He was Kathy's age. That did not matter to me. It made him seem more attractive. A man of the world ... or so I thought.

Aaron and I began dating, and I was soon in love. His plan was to leave New York to meet his best friend Jeff, who had good connections with a huge builder in Colorado. He and Jeff planned to work their way to Texas, stay a while, and gradually work their way to Colorado and get jobs with a huge construction company.

Aaron had promised me that he would "send for me" when he "got things set up." I missed him and wondered if he would keep his word "to take me away" with him. That had been many months ago. Still, I hoped one day to hear from him.

Sunday Morning

I woke up feeling chilly. It was always cool in the basement. The house was quiet. I decided to go upstairs and make coffee. I took my coffee pot with me. Lee demanded that no one else be in the kitchen while he and his family were eating. Especially at "their" dinnertime. My mother was not "allowed" in the room—banned from her own kitchen. Ridiculous. It was all so ugly.

Before Lee, Sunday mornings were a quiet joy. Mom would have her coffee at the kitchen table while she read the Sunday paper. I would lounge around in the living room and watch a morning show. Now all of that was over. We had both become prisoners in our own home. Mom spent nearly every waking hour hiding out in her bedroom—only leaving the room to work or eat.

I peered into the kitchen. No one there. I shook the old coffee grounds into the trash and rinsed out the pot. I was just filling the filter with fresh grounds when Lee came bursting into the room.

He screamed, "What do you think you are doing?" He charged at me with clenched fists and rage across his face just as he had done before.

By this time, I was determined to stop his tyrannical behavior, at least toward me. With a toss of my head, I grabbed the package of coffee and dangled it in front of him. "I'm making a pot of my coffee, Lee." He stopped dead in his tracks. His red face and flared nostrils told me that he was livid that I had dared to defy him. He had a horrible glare in his eyes and rage was all over him.

It might have been wise to keep silent, but I had seen too much, heard too much, and had put up with too much to stop now. "Let me tell you something—Lee," I pointed my finger at him as I spoke, "I was born in this house ... this is my mother's house. Do you understand ... Lee ... this is my *mother's house*. You are not in charge here!"

He stood there a few seconds. I think to this day, he was weighing whether or not to hit me. In the end, he must have decided that it would cause more problems than it was worth. For whatever reason, he turned and stormed out of the room. I finished putting the coffee on and sat at the table while I waited for it to finish perking. My mind was swimming. I realized that I had once again challenged the Warlock.

I thought about how he had tried to recruit me. His telling me about his so-called "powers." How during his "teaching speech" he had mentioned that he could move objects with his mind. I silently prayed to the Lord. I asked for courage. I knew the Lord would protect me because I carried him in my heart. I had all of heaven behind me. Still, it felt like a war ... a spiritual war.

The coffee was finished and I took a cup of it downstairs. I thought about Marilyn's words: "I wouldn't want to see you murdered, Micky." I shrugged off the thought. I would never show him any fear—never. I thought about how I had pointed my finger at him as I spoke. That was not like me, but when you have had enough bullying, you have had enough. Lee acted like a textbook bully. When confronted, he ran. I hoped it would last. However, I suspected there might come a day of reckoning for me and for Kathy—perhaps for all of us.

I decided to dress and walk to the market. There was a brutal wind but I just wanted to get the heck out of the house. It was surprisingly quiet upstairs as I left through the back door. I only had three dollars in my pocket but I knew I would take my time in the store and just buy whatever looked good.

When I got home, I went in the back door and down the stairs. I decided to do my laundry. The washer and dryer were in the hallway of the basement so I would not have to leave the confines of my makeshift subterranean bedroom. I could hear Kathy, Lee, and the kids in the kitchen. Plates clanging and dishes passing back and forth, spoons tinkling against the sides of tea glasses. What I did not hear was conversation. Talking was not "allowed." Lee insisted that everyone maintain complete silence.

Laughter and fun were a part of the "Before-Lee" life. The "After Lee" life was becoming untenable.

I never saw Lee as "good looking" and I wondered what had attracted Kathy when they met. Why did she stay? Then I remembered Marilyn's words: "She is his possession." I fought back tears as I folded my clothes.

A little later, I heard Mom come in the front door. I ran upstairs to greet her. "Hey, Mom."

"Are you alright?"

"I'm fine, Mom. Why do you ask?"

"Oh, I don't' know. Just a feeling. Your Aunt Nell sent you something."

She reached down into her purse and handed me a small box of chocolates. "Oh, how nice. Do you want a piece?"

"No, not right now, Mick. I feel tired. It's like I can never get enough rest anymore." She took a deep breath and slowly let it out through her mouth. Bending over, she picked up the bundle of newspapers on the kitchen table and headed down the hallway to her bedroom. I heard her close the door. I was not going to say anything about what had happened. It would only scare her or make her worry. She seemed worn with care. I did not want to add to it.

I was glad to go to work Monday night. It gave me something to focus on instead of my ongoing troubles with Lee. When I came home in the morning, I was surprised that both cars were gone. Mom was always gone to work by then, but Kathy and Lee's car was gone as well. I wiped my feet as I unlocked the front door and crossed the threshold. As I stepped over, I half-slipped and nearly fell into the living room. Off balance, my keys flew out of my hand and landed under the coffee table. I pulled off my coat, closed the door and got down on the floor to find my keys.

I glanced upward trying not to bang my head. I could not believe what I saw. I stopped dead. Taped to the underside of the table was a tape recorder. I also found two microphones. I jumped up and sat in the chair. "What in the world is this?" I said to no one. The table was heavy, but after a minute, I managed to clear the top and turn it on its side. I leaned the back of the table against the couch so I could get a good look at the underbelly. I stared at the equipment. That is when it all came together for me. I recalled my last day off from work, when I had heard Lee walking around the house, from the bedroom, to the kitchen, to the bedroom, to the living room. He had been moving furniture. I had also seen him with a tape recorder. He was booby trapping my mother's house.

I thought about how he had played the tape recorder with the horrible sounds on it—in and out of the bedroom window. Like a hard slap to the side of my head, it all came together. He was going to create another "haunting." I jumped out of the chair and exclaimed, "You bastard!"

I looked under the end table. Another microphone. The wire led down the inside of the leg and under the edge of the couch. I moved the coffee table to the middle of the floor and pulled the couch away from the wall. There was a wire taped to the back of the couch that led to a microphone tucked between the top of the cushions. I looked under the other end table—another microphone. This wire led to a second recorder under the couch. I stopped and sat in the chair. It is hard to express what came over me.

"Oh ... no you don't," I shouted. "This will not happen in my mother's house. You will not make her a part of your evil scheme."

My world changed in that instant. This foolish, evil man had already ruined my sister's life. He was not going to ruin my mother's life. I ran into the kitchen and grabbed a large trash bag. Back in the living room, I began ripping out the microphone from under the end table. Next came the mic and wires from the back of the couch. I shoved it all into the trash bag. Recorders, mics, wires …they all were ripped from their place of concealment and thrown into the ballooning trash bag.

After removing all the electronics I could find, I pushed the couch and tables back where they belonged. To be safe, I decided to check the other furniture in the room. The television set caught my eye. I crawled over to look underneath the set. It looked like some kind of a lens—a camera lens. I reached my hand under the set and tried to pull it out but it was too big. I pulled the television away from the wall. The camera was large and it looked expensive. I had never seen one like it. Into the trash bag. My heart was beating like a bomb but the living room was "clean" and swept of devices.

I dragged the trash bag into the kitchen. I had heard him moving things around in the kitchen as well. Sure enough, there was another tape recorder and two microphones taped to the bottom of the kitchen table. I climbed under the table and ripped them off. Into the bag it went. I checked the rest of the room and found another camera behind the stereo. It was set with the lens facing out, toward the middle of the room. Into the bag. I put my coat and gloves on and picked up the heavy trash bag. Before going outside to dispose of the "equipment," I took one last look to make sure that everything was in place.

The front door closed behind me. I checked the lock. My arms strained to carry the bag. I walked up the block and turned the first corner, then three more blocks north, then two blocks west to the main drag. The first commercial dumpster I came to was in front of a diner. I heaved the bag into the dumpster and lowered the lid, then headed back to the house. I knew all that equipment had to be expensive. I realized as I walked that Lee, once he discovered the missing equipment, would know I had taken it. Who else would touch it? As I walked, both fear and defiance swept over me in alternating waves. I had always wondered why he chose to stay at my Mom's house after he and Kathy left the Amityville house in such a hurry.

Lee's parents were "well-off" and owned a big house. I had been there. So why had he been so keen on moving everyone into Mom's house? Now I understood. He had chosen Mom's house because he thought he could get away with whatever he wanted in her house. He believed that no one would question him or dare to accuse him of rigging a "haunting." Perhaps he assumed his parents would not be so easily fooled.

Lee had taken over my mom's house—he was completely in charge. He instilled fear in everyone. But not me. I had discovered his dirty little secret and he would never intimidate me again.

I decided that if he asked me anything I would simply tell him, "I threw it all away." What could he do? Nothing. When I got back, no one was home. I was glad. I could not have handled another confrontation with Lee.

I checked the living room and kitchen once more to be sure they were right. Everything looked normal, so I went downstairs to my bedroom. I had been awake for hours and yet I was not tired. Still, I had to get some sleep. I put on my nightshirt and pulled back the covers. It felt good to lay down. The alarm was set for one p.m. I had a full night's work ahead of me.

It had been an eventful day, and one that I knew I would never forget. I also knew that once Lee discovered what I had done, he would never forget either. Nevertheless, I could not worry about that now. I was glad that I had squelched his evil plans.

As I drifted off to sleep, I kept thinking about how crazy my life and the rest of my family's lives had become. Completely crazy. What do evil people do when you foil their best-laid plans? I had no idea, but somehow I suspected that eventually, I would find out the price of resisting evil. As it turned out, I had no idea how bad it could be.

Family home in West Babylon, N.Y., where Kathy and I grew up; 1961.

My mother, Johanna Conners, in the snow in front of our West Babylon house; 1960.

(Left to right)My sister, Kathy Conners Lutz , me, my mother, Johanna Conners; 1991.

Mom and I on Sunday morning,
1964.

Micky (right) and my friend Debbie on Easter day, May 1960. I was four-years-old.

Kathy and a friend at home in West Babylon.
Kathy was sixteen, 1962.

Kathy and her soon-to-be husband, Seb, on their graduation day; June 1964.

CHAPTER TEN

the fatal flaw

The next two days rolled by. I kept to myself. The equipment had been gone for 48 hours. No one had said a word about the missing recording devices. *Did Lee even know that the cameras and audio equipment were no longer there?* I had decided that if he asked me about the equipment, I would tell him that I had thrown it all in a dumpster. I planned to tell him why. No one, not George Lee Lutz, or anyone else was going to turn my mother's home and all of lives into some kind of circus, to make money for Lee.

I thought he might come at me physically again, like he had done before in the kitchen, but I was *not* afraid. I had stood up to him before and I would do it again.

The third morning after I had removed the equipment, I woke up startled. I could hear Lee yelling upstairs. He sounded like he was in a rage. I ran up the stairs. Had he discovered the surveillance equipment was gone?

As I entered the kitchen, I could see Lee standing in front of my mother, his face was red, his body rigid. He had both hands on Mom's thin upper-arms. His knuckles gleamed white against her dark-blue shirt. Too many times, I had seen him grab Kathy that way.

He began dragging Mom down the hallway, gripping one arm; he opened her bedroom door and shoved her inside. He quickly slammed the door, and yelled at her, "Don't even think about coming out of that room!" Then he stomped back to his bedroom. He had not seen me standing around the corner.

I walked to Mom's bedroom door. I could hear her crying. I knew this was not the moment to ask her what had happened. I quietly went back downstairs. *How dare he attack my mother ... touch her like that!*

My mind raced. Was it about the equipment? Did he discover I had removed it? Was he blaming Mom? I muttered the words aloud. "You evil bastard." A few moments later I heard Mom leave for work.

My anger had reached a crescendo. I was convinced that George Lee Lutz was an ever-present danger. I heard myself say the words softly, "You're a dead man." I did not know how I was going to do it, but I knew that if something did not stop him, he was going to hurt us.

Hurt us all.

That night I decided not to go to work. I was too upset and too worried. I went upstairs and called my boss. The phone cord reached into the bathroom where I placed the call. I did not want to be overheard. I told my boss that I was not well and would not be coming to work that night.

"You are a good worker, Mick. Stay home, take it easy, and get better. I will see you tomorrow," he said.

Something had to change.

Later that day the house was empty. After several minutes had passed and the house remained quiet, I went upstairs and put on a pot of coffee. The smell of the coffee made me long for my old life, before George had met my sister. As incredible as it sounded, even to me, I realized that I would have to kill him. Someone has to save them. I would have to kill the Warlock.

At that moment I remembered my boyfriend Aaron's words just before he left New York to go establish a place in Texas, "If you need anything Mick, while I'm gone, call this guy. His name is Ronnie and I have already told him that you might call if you need something." I never thought I would need it so I just took the note and stuffed it into a pocket of my purse. Maybe Ronnie could help.

I had been carrying the note in my purse since Aaron had given it to me. After tearing everything out of my purse and dumping it on the table, I found Ronnie's number.

Aaron's words echoed in my head, "No matter what you need, Mick, call Ronnie. He can help you." With a new determination and the will to make a change, I went to the kitchen and dialed the number.

After four rings, a man answered. "Hello."

"Hi, I am looking for Ronnie. Is your name Ronnie?" I asked.

"Who's this?"

My name is Micky, and I am Aaron O' Reilly's girlfriend. He gave me your number before he left. He told me that if I ever needed anything, you could help."

"Yeah, sure."

"Can you loan me a gun?"

He paused, but then said, "Ugh ... where are you?" I gave him Mom's address.

"Give me thirty minutes, Micky. I will meet you near Straight Path in thirty minutes, at the end of the block."

I glanced at the clock. Straight Path was the name of the main drag at the far end of our block. I ran downstairs, threw my clothes on, and grabbed my big winter coat and gloves. I pulled the hood of my coat over my head as tightly as I could as I went out the back door. It was raining buckets. I half-ran and half-walked up the street. I got there before Ronnie and it gave me time to think. I was not sure what I was going to do with the gun, but at least I would no longer be without any protection from the evil presence that had hijacked my family. A few minutes later, a car pulled off the main street and turned onto our block. The driver leaned across the front seat, to the passenger side and rolled down the window "Micky?" He called out.

"Yeah ... Ronnie?" He motioned me toward the car. I got in. He was twenty-something, dark-haired and not bad looking. I recognized him. I had met him once at a barbeque that Aaron and I had visited.

Without a word, he reached into the back seat and placed a rifle on my lap. It seemed enormous. Then he popped open the glove box and handed me a box.

"Are these bullets?" I asked.

He laughed and said, "You call these *cartridges*, but yes ... they are the "bullets" for this rifle." He sat back and smiled at me. "Do you know how to use this?"

"Not really," I said as I looked at him like a deer in the headlights.

He laughed. "I'll show you." With that, he took two cartridges from the box and showed me how to open the rifle. "This is called a twelve-gauge, double-barreled, sawed-off shotgun. When you load these cartridges in here, close the rifle like this." The rifle snapped shut. "You cock it like this. Once it is loaded, it is ready to fire. Do you think you can do that?"

"Can you show me just once more?" He laughed and nodded his head.

I paid close attention as he went through the process of loading the gun one more time. "Do I owe you any money ... for the gun, I mean?"

He said, "Well I owe your guy so this one's on the house."

"Thank you Ronnie, I hope I won't need to use this thing, but I feel better knowing I have it."

"When you're finished with the rifle, call me at the same number and I'll meet you back here to get it."

As I stepped out of the car, I struggled to get the rifle and the box under my coat.

Before I closed the door he said, "Be careful with that, it's a hit-man's gun with a hair-trigger."

"Thanks, Ronnie."

He gave me a quick nod as the car spun around and went back toward the main drag. It was still pouring rain. I had to hold tightly to the rifle and the box under my coat, but I managed.

I walked as fast as I could back to the house and went straight downstairs. I was soaked to the bone. I took the shotgun and the box out from under my coat and set them down. My coat was dripping wet. I hung it up next to the oil burner where I knew it would dry quickly. The shotgun was so big. I had never held a gun before in my life. I picked it up and went through the motions he had shown me. "Open it—load it—close it—cock it." That is what Ronnie had told me to do. I did this several times. After I felt comfortable, or at least as comfortable as I could feel, I hid the shotgun and the box under the cushions of the couch. I thought about how he had warned me about the "hair-trigger." I was not sure what that meant, but I had a feeling it had something to do with the ease of shooting off a round of ammunition.

No one was home, but it was still early. Because I had never fired a gun, I knew that I needed to find a place where I could practice. Not too far from my house, there was an old abandoned area. Three of the houses had burned, leaving only the shells. There was nothing around them but woods for several blocks. No one went there.

I changed into some dry clothes, pulled the shotgun and box of shells from under the couch cushions. I put four cartridges into my pants pocket, slipped a small jacket on and then my big coat over it. The shotgun stuffed under my coat. I walked out the back door. It was still cold, but the rain had stopped. I pulled the hood of my coat over my head. I did not want people to see my face.

I walked the half-mile to the abandoned houses. To get to them I had to fight my way through the trees and chest-high weeds that had grown up around them. After a minute or two, the undergrowth thinned, and I could see the partial roof on one of the burned-out houses. I could see or hear no one.

The shotgun was heavy in my hand. I pulled two cartridges from my pocket and loaded it. I closed and cocked it, and pressed the butt of the shotgun into my shoulder as hard as I could. I aimed at a portion of a wall that was in front of me. I reached with my index finger to the trigger and lightly touched it.

"Boom."

The impact knocked me off my feet. My shoulder ached. It felt and sounded like a cannon. I looked at the hole in the wall in disbelief—it was huge. My ears were ringing and I had hardly touched the trigger. The true meaning of "hair-trigger" had become abundantly clear. Fear gripped me as I wondered if someone else might have heard the blast. After opening the gun and checking the chamber to make sure it was not loaded, I slipped it back beneath my coat and made my way to the street.

Feeling more confident about using the firearm and seeing how much damage it could do, I walked back to the house. I went downstairs and hid the shotgun and the cartridges. I took off my coat and sat down on the couch. The blanket across the back of the couch felt good as I covered my body. My shoulder still hurt from the blast. I was miserable. Some sleep would be good.

Several hours had passed. I could hear the shower running upstairs. Everyone must be back home. I ran up the stairs to the back door and looked out onto the driveway. It was almost dawn. Mother was getting ready for work. I listened as I heard her walk to her bedroom, then a few minutes later, the front door slammed shut. Mom had left for work.

Minutes later, I heard heavy footsteps from the bedroom to the bathroom. It was Lee. I knew his heavy, slow gate. This was my chance. I took the shotgun out loaded it, and snapped it shut. The heavy footsteps moved from the bathroom into the kitchen. I held the shotgun in my hands. A silent prayer came from my lips:

"Forgive me God, for what I am about to do."

It was my life in exchange for the safety of my family.

My plan was to do what I had to do, then call the police. My feet, covered in soft thick socks allowed me to ascend the stairs without detection. When I reached the top step, I quietly stepped into the kitchen. Lee's back was towards me. He was making his "coffee" at the stove as he did every morning. I silently pressed my back against the wall and moved the shotgun to my hip—pointed towards his back. The end of the barrel was less than five-feet from him. I knew I would not miss.

My finger was poised next to the trigger when Kathy's voice called out from the bedroom. Her voice was pleading. "Leeeee ... Leeeee ...." Lee turned and walked toward the bedroom as though he never saw me.

I thought about it for a second. Did he know I was there? As I ran the scene back in my mind, I realized that he took a full step sideways before he turned to walk into the bedroom. In that second, after Kathy called his name, perhaps he "knew" that I was behind him and why. My moment had passed. I silently crept down the stairs, unloaded the gun and put it under the couch cushions.

My face was wet with perspiration and my hands shook. I grabbed a towel and pressed it to my face. I cried uncontrollably as I begged God to forgive me for what I had almost done. I was never a violent person. I had never even hit anyone. Even though I felt shame and guilt, I also realized I had squandered the best chance I might ever have of ridding our family of this evil entity. My hands shook as I cried out to the Lord, "Forgive me, Lord." As the perspiration faded, and my hands stopped shaking, I knew in my heart, that I would never do such a thing again. I was not a killer. There had to be another way.

Hours later, I heard them leave the house. The house was empty once more so I took the opportunity to go upstairs and get a shower. It was a work-night and I looked forward to being as far away as I could manage from this troubled house.

The next morning I returned the shotgun at the same meeting place. Ronnie did not ask me any questions. As Ronnie sped away, I was relieved. No more shotgun … no more thinking about ending someone's life. I never wanted to feel that way again.

On the walk home, I thanked the Lord for protecting me. I decided that if Lee touched my mother again I would call the police. I thought it was odd—did Mr. I-Can-See-Your-Thoughts really have no idea that I was standing behind him, aiming a shotgun at his back. That sidestep he took before he turned spoke volumes to me. I believe he knew that I was there. If nothing else, at least it proved he was scared, that is why he took the side step.

The week passed quietly, without incident. No one asked me about anything. Still no mention of the missing equipment.

Several Days Later

I came home from work to find Kathy was alone in the kitchen. I stood close to her and half whispered, "Kathy is it true that a book is being written about what happened in the Amityville house?" She looked at me and nodded. Her face looked tense but she was smiling. "Yes,

Mick, they are going to write a book about the time we spent in that awful house." I nodded my head and began to step away, but she grabbed my arm and said, "Wait a minute, Mick. I need to tell you something. Lee does not want your name mentioned. He made me promise that you would have nothing to do with this project. I hope you understand Micky, but this is the way it has to be."

"So? Don't worry about it Kathy, I am fine with that." There was no point in arguing with her and besides, I knew that anything Lee said to her was law.

Of course, he did not want my name mentioned. If I ever told anyone, what I knew it would blow his whole innocent-Christian-victim horror story, right out of the water. He considered me a threat, and for good reason. I knew what George Lee Lutz was capable of doing. I alone knew the level of deception, manipulation, and control he practiced. He knew that given the chance, I could expose him as an occult figure, a warlock, and a fraud.

dream stalker

Saturday afternoon I had showered and stepped from the bathroom in my robe. A towel wrapped around my head like a turban. As I headed down the stairs, the phone rang, and since I was right there, I was able to answer it before anyone else got to it. Lee did not like anyone to answer the phone. He wanted to control all incoming messages. It was part of his plan for total domination.

"Hello." I said into the receiver. I could not believe the voice on the other end.

"Hey baby, how ya doing?"

For a moment I thought I was dreaming, "Aaron ... is that you?"

"Well yeah ... it's me," he replied. I was in shock. After all this time, Aaron was calling me. He had been gone for months.

"Where are you? I haven't heard from you in a long time. I miss you."

"Mick, do you remember when I left that I told you I would send for you when I got things ready?"

"Yeah, I remember."

"Well, guess what? I am in Texas right now—just as I promised. Mick, I'm buying you a ticket to meet me here. You can fly out tomorrow morning."

"Are you kidding me?" Aaron explained that his best friend Jeff was with him. He told me that two other couples that we knew from New York and his sister were already driving to meet "us" in Texas. From there we were all going to Colorado where Jeff had an old friend from his army days who could get the guys good jobs. He told me not to worry and gave me the airline and ticket information. Then he told me that if I needed a ride to the airport he would send one of his brothers to take me.

"I'll ask Mom to take me," I told him.

He gave me a phone number to call him right back and let him know. I ran to Mom's room and told her everything. I ran back to the phone to call him back. When he answered. I said, "Mom's taking me."

"Well ... baby, I'll see you tomorrow." I ran downstairs and combed out my wet hair, looked at my pile of dirty clothes and threw them into the washing machine. I could hardly think. *Tomorrow. I am leaving to meet Aaron—in Texas.* It hardly seemed real.

As I threw my clothes into the dryer, I realized that I did not have a suitcase. Mom found one for me in the back of her closet. I was beginning a new life, away from Lutz and his crazy-scary self.

I ran down the hall from Mom's room lugging the empty suitcase. Kathy and Lee were sitting on the living room couch. I stopped and exclaimed, "I'm going to Texas tomorrow." Kathy looked surprised and Lee just glared at me.

I do not care what Kathy or Lee think—I am out of here.

Each piece of clothing I folded from the dryer went straight into the suitcase. My mind dreamed of where I was going. I set aside my best shirt and jeans. The hours seemed to fly. As I looked around my room, I realized I did not have much to take. A radio, an alarm clock, and some books. I picked out a few of my favorite Christian books and stuffed them into the suitcase. I was packed. Mom called down, "Soup and a sandwich, Micky. Come and get something to eat." I was starving. After lunch, I cleaned the table and did the dishes, then went downstairs to finish packing.

I checked my room then double-checked to make sure I had everything I needed. The house was dark and quiet. I stood there and thought about how much I loved my Mom and Kathy and the kids. Tears streamed down my face. I quietly kissed each of the kids as they slept and whispered, "I love you."

The next morning, Mom called downstairs, "I'll be in the car, Micky. It's time to go to the airport." I threw my coat on and grabbed the suitcase. Before I left, I wanted to tell Kathy goodbye and give her a hug. Lee stood like a human barricade to their bedroom. His arms placed on either side of the doorway, Kathy peeked under his arm as she stood behind him. She would not move beyond his outstretched arms. I stepped closer and stood on my tiptoes so I could see my sister's face. "Kathy, I'm leaving now. Just remember how much I love you. Take care of yourself and the kids."

"Always," she said. I could see the tears welling in her eyes. All I could think about was being free of this house and the bondage of George Lee Lutz. I turned and walked out.

As I got into the car Mom exclaimed, "We have to hurry or you'll miss your plane." As we drove, I could not help but wonder why Lee had stopped me from saying goodbye to my sister. It was just another way to control her. To keep us apart and to keep her isolated. I felt sorry for her, but realized, that until she understood the terrible evil that had gripped her and her family, there was nothing I, or anyone else, could do to loosen the hold he had on her.

I reached over and touched Mom's shoulder. "I love you, Mom."

"I know, Mick."

In no time, we were at the airport. Mom came with me as we headed for the boarding area. Before I left, I held her tight. "I love you so much, Mom."

"I just want to say one thing Mick. I have never seen you as happy as I do at this moment. But, just remember this ... He's a *Romeo*." I did not understand her comment at the time, but I did not question her. I was too happy to be leaving to be with the man of my dreams. If I had asked Mom to explain her "Romeo" comment, I am sure she would have refused. I was too young to accept or fully understand her advice. She knew that—I did not.

"Call me and let me know when you get there." She turned and disappeared into the crowd. Determined to leave, I headed toward the loading area. However, Mother's words still rang in my head. "Romeo," she had said. I fought back tears as I boarded the plane and within moments, we were lifting off. As I looked out the window, I watched as New York City disappeared below me.

It was surreal. As the plane climbed through the clouds, so did my heart. I decided that I would never say anything about all that had happened. I did not want to think about it anymore. My life was changing. I wanted to leave all the evil behind me. Especially Lee. I was flying away from my troubles. At least that is what I thought at the time. Little did I realize that a young woman's dreams are like waves upon the ocean … each one will strike upon the shore and soak into the sand … forever gone. The evil was not finished with me yet, and my mother's words would prove to be prophetic.

It was the summer of '76 and I thought the world was mine. We had stayed in a small travel-trailer for a month before leaving Texas. Then Aaron, me, and his friend Jeff and Jeff's girlfriend, Pat and another couple we knew in New York, Dennis and Laura made it to Colorado.

I knew that I would make Colorado my home right away. I loved it. Aaron and I found a nice apartment and settled in. One day while walking home from the grocery store, I felt very tired and decided to stop along the roadside and rest. We lived in a quiet neighborhood in Montrose. It was a beautiful place, and the city maintained a lovely park-like atmosphere. I saw a black metal park bench beside the sidewalk. I had two heavy bags of groceries in my arms. I stopped to sit a few minutes and catch my breath.

As I looked around the neighborhood, I wondered how Kathy and the kids were doing. I had spoken to Mom once a week since I had been gone, but she never wanted to say much about Kathy and she refused to discuss George.

Still sitting on the bench and lost in my thoughts of home, I noticed a glimmer of something shiny lying behind the foot of the bench. I reached down to see what it might be. A silver necklace lay coiled in a circle. On the thin silver chain hung a beautiful silver-dove pendant. The chain was unbroken. I knew exactly what it was. I placed it around my neck and smiled to myself—a sign.

Feeling better, I stood and retrieved my two bags of groceries and walked the two blocks to my house. As I put away the groceries, someone knocked on the front door. When I opened the door, a middle-aged woman stood in front of me. Her hair was long, longer than fashionable for an "older" woman. Her dress was mid-calf length, and her shoes were nothing short of "sensible." She had what appeared to be a Bible in her hand and some brochures, one of which I felt sure she was going to leave with me.

"Hi," she said. "My name is Evelyn and I am a Jehovah's Witness ... Church of the Latter Day Saints. Have you heard of us?"

"Yes, but I don't know much about your religion. I am a Christian."

"I couldn't help but notice your necklace ... the beautiful dove ... do you know the significance of that dove?"

"Yes I do know its significance," I told her. "It's the dove that landed on Jesus's head when he was baptized in the Jordon River by John the Baptist." With that, she handed me some literature and walked away with a smile.

As I closed the door, and walked back to the kitchen to finish putting away the groceries, I passed the hallway mirror and stopped to admire my newly acquired necklace. It was so beautiful. I wore that necklace for several years and it was always a source of comfort to me.

It was 1978 and I did not know it at the time, but it would be a tumultuous year in my life.

Aaron and I had been living together since that fateful day that I left New York to meet him. We were still hanging out with the same group of friends. We had all thrown our fortunes together to make a new life in Colorado.

The previous year, I had spoken to my father by phone. Communication with my dad was rare and I cherished the attention that he gave me; like the Thanksgiving card that he had sent to me in early November 1977. He had signed the card: "I love you, Dad." I was thrilled.

We spoke several times on the phone during the Christmas holidays and through the spring of '78. He had agreed to come out to see me that March. I was like a middle-school kid on her first date: scared, hoping things would go well during his visit, and wanting our relationship to be better than it had been when I lived in New York.

Since he was planning to stay a few days, I got busy preparing the spare bedroom so he would not have to get a hotel room. I had freshly painted the room and I added a new comforter, pillows, and curtains for the windows. I was ready. I could not wait for my father to arrive. As far as I was concerned, we were going to be "good friends." This was going to be a "new start" with my dad who was absent through too much of my childhood. In those days, he spent his weekends in bars, hanging out with his "drinking buddies" instead of his family. He and Mom fought many times, about his drinking. Those fights always became physical. I wanted to put all of that behind me and make new memories with Dad, peaceful memories.

That night I had a disturbing dream. A dream about my father. He was standing in a wide field, and he was reaching out to me. I was standing on the other side of the field, reaching back toward him. I could not move from where I was standing. I was rooted there, and so was he. He just kept reaching, but neither of us moved. I assumed it was a representational dream, not a prophetic one. In the dream, the field represented the distance between us both physically and emotionally. We could not reach each other because we needed to learn how to become "Dad and daughter."

The morning of March 4, I jumped out of bed and began to get ready for the big visit. Dad was due in that morning on an early flight. I only had twenty minutes to get to the airport. However, that was not a problem. I only lived five minutes from the airport.

I checked the house for last details, grabbed my jacket and my purse and headed for the door. Just before I closed the door, I heard the phone ringing. "I better get it, it might be something important," I muttered to myself as I laid my keys on the hall table. "Hello," I said. It was Mom.

"Mick, I have some bad news for you ... you're father's dead."

"What?"

"You're father's dead ... Micky," she repeated.

"But I'm on my way to the airport; he'll be here in a few minutes! Mom, this cannot be true ... maybe it's a mistake."

"Micky, your father is dead and that's that. I'll call you later."

How could she just hang-up without telling me what happened? I was dumbstruck. I stood frozen, listening to the dead-tone on the phone still in my hand. "Surely, she must be wrong," I said to myself as I locked the front door and headed to the airport.

The passengers disembarked one by one. The woman with her little boy who looked like he had been sleeping on the plane. The man with the black leather briefcase, wearing a frown and a crumpled white dress-shirt. The young woman, no more than twenty, looking expectantly down the gang walk for someone who was there to meet her.

Not yet.

I watched each passenger leave the plane. Dad was not there. I drove home and sat in a state of disbelief. We would never get the chance to be "friends." It was too late for me.

At my father's wake, I waited until everyone left the room. I took a red rose from one of the floral vases, and then removed my treasured dove necklace. I placed the rose and necklace into my father's hand and said, "Dad, this is the dove that landed on Jesus' head. Know that I love you, Dad. Go to the Lord and be at peace."

***

Many months later, I inherited a sum of money—almost three-thousand dollars. It was from savings bonds that my mother had insisted on buying and saving. It was a wonderful gift from my father and more money than I had ever known. I wanted to use it for something important. I decided that buying a small house would put that money to good use and ensure a solid future for me.

A local bank approved a loan and I became a first-time homeowner. It was thrilling. The house was tiny, only one bedroom, but to me it was a mansion. At the end of the block, there was the city park. It was "home." I was never so proud in my life. *I own a home,* I thought to myself. Aaron and I moved in and I continued to work my job at the pharmacy downtown, on Main Street. The world was mine. I was happy, even though it still made me sad that Dad would never see my beautiful house. Aaron and I had been a couple for a few years. I was sure he would ask me to marry him now that we had moved into the house.

He had asked me to plan on a dinner-out the following Saturday night. I was excited because I knew that he was going to ask me the "big question."

The town we lived in was small. There were only two restaurants. I did not care where we had dinner. I was too excited. I just wanted to be married and live in my little house with my new husband. It had not been an easy relationship. Aaron worked steady in the carpet laying business, but he went out a lot and I had always suspected that he ran around with other women. I believed that once we were "married" he would settle down and become a faithful husband. I ignored my mother's admonition … "watch out for him, Mick. He's a Romeo." Mother's know these things, but daughters do not listen.

I said, "Yes" to Aaron's proposal of marriage believing he would stop running around. Two weeks after we were married, I came home from work and found the house empty.

All that remained was my bedframe and mattress. My clothes were on the closet floor and my dog Butchie was still in the yard. All of the living room furniture was gone. No towels, no sheets, no blankets and no dishes. Everything was gone. I was bewildered, scared, and confused. *Where is he? Why is everything gone?*

Two days later, his best friend, Jeff knocked on the door. "Hey, Micky ... I know that you are probably confused right now. I want you to know that the only reason he married you was that he wanted your house and your car. If ... when ... you see Aaron, do not tell him I was here. Okay?"

I swallowed hard. His words were harsh, but he was telling me what I already knew. Aaron was no good. He was out for "Aaron" and for no one else.

I filed for divorce and the judge gave him neither my house, nor my car. I had managed to avoid another disaster. I really hoped that my bad luck was over.

***

Months went by and I became accustomed to being alone and going to work every day. My job at the pharmacy was steady and the pay was good enough. I could live for now. I had escaped a warlock's clutches in New York, and now I was free of a philandering husband. What could possibly go wrong?

In the world of the occult, there is "no time or distance." George Lee Lutz had said that to me once, long ago. During his speech to try to recruit me with his "teaching offer." Unfortunately I would soon learn what he meant by "no time or space."

CHAPTER TWELVE

the curse

1981

Time seemed to fly by as I continued my job at the drug store. Life was a real struggle just to feed my dog, myself, and pay the bills, but I had made peace with Aaron leaving and being on my own. I was accomplishing something, moving forward and making things happen. My dream was to one day give this house to Mom and Aunt Nell. I could earn another house for myself.

I continued to pay on the house and put a few dollars in my savings account. One Sunday, I realized that I had forgotten to check my mailbox on Saturday. There was a letter—addressed to me. I never got mail. Only bills. I had not spoken to Kathy since I had left New

York. Lee would not allow her to talk to the family, except to call Mom occasionally. She was afraid of him. She did as told—exactly.

Although there was no return address, I recognized the handwriting immediately. It was Kathy's handwriting, which was very distinctive. My heart leaped. Finally, a letter from my big sister. Mom must have given Kathy my address. How else could she have known where I was living? I was so excited. I placed the letter on my kitchen table and ran to feed my dog. I wanted to be able to concentrate on reading my sister's letter without the dog howling for her supper.

The dog fed, I pulled off my coat and sat down. I stared at the letter, but did not open it right away. Just to see her handwriting on the envelope was such a thrill. I opened it slowly, being careful not to tear the envelope and destroy any of the writing. Inside of the envelope was one page of white paper folded into thirds. I unfolded the first third. Too late, I realized that it was not a letter from my sister at all. *Her* handwriting on the outside was a decoy ... it was *Lee's* handwriting on the inside letter. The letter blatantly said that if I did not do what it said, including rebuking God that I would be dead in 24 hours.

I leaped from the chair and threw the letter down on the table. This cannot be happening. He cannot harm me now; I am all the way across the country. It was then that his words to me so long ago rang in my head: "Evil knows no time, space, or distance." It was Lutz the Warlock. He had sent me the letter in hopes of controlling me and ruining my new life I had made for myself. My hands were shaking, but I had to read it one more time. It was when I read it again, that the anger began to rise up in me and starve out the fear. He cannot do this to me, I thought. He will not do this to me. I held the letter high above my head as I stood in my kitchen. I lifted my right hand towards heaven, as I yelled aloud, "Father God, Almighty! I know this is not your word!"

With that, I lowered my hand and walked to my kitchen garbage pail. I ripped the letter apart. Piece by piece, strip by strip, it fluttered into the garbage. With each rip, I said these words: "In the power of the name of the Lord Jesus Christ, I rebuke these words!" I grabbed the envelope, tore it up and it too fell into in the garbage. My hands still trembling, I walked into my bedroom and sat down on my bed.

My head was swimming. *It is a curse ... the Warlock has sent me a curse.* Surely, Kathy did not know about what was inside that envelope. I thought about the power and control he held over her. My heart ached to believe that my sister did not know what Lee had written on that paper. In my heart, I believe that she did not know.

I speculated that Lee was afraid that I might tell someone all that I knew about him and his plan for the Amityville hoax. The curse was to ensure my silence. What he did not know was that I loved my sister far too much to divulge his dirty little secret. I knew that if I ever said anything while the warlock was around, her life could be in the balance. I would never do anything to hurt or endanger her. I never wanted to tell anyone what I knew.

My hope was that Kathy and the kids were okay and he had not done anything to harm them, at least not more than the harm he had already done—to all of them, including my mother. My feelings were overwhelming. Anger and fear. I was angry that the Warlock thought he could frighten me and sad at how much I missed Kathy and the kids.

That night, I wrestled to fall asleep. My day began at 6 a.m. After many restless hours I fell asleep at five; the alarm sounded at six, and the noise startled me out of a deep sleep. I got up, threw on my robe, and went to the kitchen. It was almost dawn. I put on some coffee and let it brew while I ran a quick bath. Installing a shower was my next project for the house. I have always loved a hot bath. The water was steaming as I took off my robe and sat on the edge of the tub. I dipped my hand into the partially filled tub and the water felt hot, but not scalding. I leaned over to turn off the water, and that is when it hit me. The pain struck in my chest. Foolishly, I climbed into the tub. That is when the real pain came, like a hammer thrown into my chest. A lightning-bolt pain zinged through my side. I could not move but I knew I had to get out of that water. The pain, which had started in my rib cage, had gravitated up my chest. I could not breathe. The muscles felt so tight I could barely move.

I had no way of knowing at the time, but I would later find out that my right lung had collapsed. The collapsed lung was crushing my heart. Instinct took over. I slithered my wet body across the side of the tub as I fell on the floor in a dripping mass. My breathing was incredibly shallow. It was all I could do to take in any breath at all. I did the best I could to wrap my gown around me as I crawled to the front door. I was able to pull myself up with the help of the door handle and get to my feet.

Once outside, I grasped each tree for a second as I made my way down the driveway. I stumbled across the empty street and knocked on the neighbor's front door. There were lights on. A woman opened the door. "Oh, my God, you can't breathe can you?" I shook my head. "You need to go to the hospital don't you?" I shook my head again. She grabbed me into her arms and sat me in a chair. She yelled to her son, "Jason, get the truck. Hurry. This woman needs a hospital. Now." Jason ran into the living room, scooped me up into his arms and carried me to the truck. He placed me in the passenger's side. We made it to the emergency room in record time.

In the process of getting me to the hospital, my nightgown had fallen away. The ER nurses put me on the stretcher and wheeled me into ER. I was naked, lying on a table. I was beyond caring and just wanted some relief from the incredible pain. Two doctors and two nurses worked on me. They did not give me painkillers or anesthetic. No time. A scalpel. The doctor cut a two-inch hole into my right side. He held what looked like a harpoon gun—pointed at me. The end of the "harpoon" had a pointed blade while the other end had a one-inch diameter plastic hose attached to it.

They inserted the bladed end into the hole in my side, then they both pushed with what seemed to be all their might. I felt the hose ripping through me. A giant gush of air came from my body. It sounded like a bicycle tire suddenly going flat. One doctor hooked the end of the hose to a machine, which was beside my gurney.

"I'm sorry," The doctor said, "but we had no time. We had to use the injection rod."

"Can you tell me your name?" He asked.

I could not get the words out. "Don't worry," he said, "we'll talk later." He gave me a shot the nurse had prepared and the pain lessened. I was freezing. A nurse covered me with a blanket.

Moments later, they took me to another room where they x-rayed my chest and upper body. Once done, someone pushed me out into the hallway. A doctor came up to me and asked, "Was it your neighbor that brought you in?

I nodded, yes.

"Well, he went home and came back … he said his mother went into your house and they brought back your purse."

"Is your name Mildred…," he said, as he looked at my driver's license, "Mildred … Conners?" I nodded. "Well at least we've established who you are. I need to know how this happened. Your right lung has ruptured and crushed your heart. Can you tell me what you were doing when this happened?" He leaned closely with his ear close to my mouth.

I mustered the word "bath."

He leaned back with a puzzled expression on his face.

"Bath? Are you trying to tell me you were taking a bath when this happened?" He shook his head and rested his fingers on his chin. "But that doesn't make any sense—it doesn't happen that way. This is very unusual. We need to do surgery tomorrow morning. I am going to construct a wall that should protect your heart. Because if this happens again, you will not live through it. Do you understand?" I nodded.

A nurse wheeled me into a room and administered an I.V. Then she gave me a shot and told me to "try and rest." Mercifully, I drifted off.

The next thing that I knew, I was aware that I was in surgery. I could hear the doctor. He was giving orders but I did not understand what he was saying.

I could feel every inch of the incision as he opened my body to begin the process of "building a wall inside my chest to protect my heart." It began under my right breast and went all the way around and up into my back. The shape of a fish's gill. When the surgeon made the incision, I felt my mind rise up as though a few inches in front of my face. I heard myself scream. A scream so terrible I cannot describe it. That was the last thing I remembered about the surgery. Knives full of fire. There were no lights. There were no tunnels. Many other people were around me. Waiting. We were laying in rows. The Lord was passing slowly through each row. As he came near me, he said in a very still quiet voice. "Get up now." I instantly began rushing forward. Faster than any roller coaster that you can imagine.

The closer I moved forward the colder it became. Progressively colder, then colder still. I had never felt such a cold. Then, as suddenly as the rushing sensation began, it stopped. It was quiet; I had the feeling of standing completely still. No movement at all. I opened my eyes. There were no lights in the room. As my eyes adjusted and I began to reorient myself, I realized that there was a space at the bottom of a closed door behind me. The bright light behind the door beamed inside the room from the one-inch crack at the bottom. The light from that space illuminated the room where I lay.

I was on a steel table. It was terribly cold. I was wearing a hospital gown. The wall in front of me was made of cinder block. A vent cover was in the top right-hand corner of the ceiling. The cover was the same size as the blocks beside it. The painted walls were an acid green, which gave everything in the room an unearthly green hue. I made a mental inventory of my body: legs, arms, back, and chest. My right arm had no feeling. The flesh of my arm had a purple, bluish-gray hue. My fingernails were purple. The creases of my knuckles looked black. My feet and lower legs were gray-purple.

Tubes ran along the table and seemed to go inside my body. There source was a square machine with lights on the front. Someone had placed it there beside my table. My right arm stretched to its full length, and lay at a forty-five degree angle from my body. I knew that I needed to get off the table. First, I would have to sit up.

It took me a quite a while to struggle into a sitting position. I could tell there was a large wound under the bandage on my right side. I reached across my body with my left hand and felt the bandages.

When I looked to my right, I saw a man lying on a table beside me. He looked long and thin. His dark, curly hair was unwashed. The sadness over-took me—he would never leave this room. He was dead. On the table next to him, there was a second body, covered by a sheet. Grey-colored feet and toes peeked out from under the sheet. They were a man's feet. Beside "toes," was a fourth table—it was empty. I knew we were in the morgue. I needed to get out.

The machine was on wheels. I grabbed the tubing with my left hand and gently pulled, slowly pulling it closer to me. Leaning on the machine with my left arm, I was able to try to stand. With a little more effort, and hanging on to the machine for dear life, I got to my feet—my balance hopelessly compromised. I knew that wherever I was going from here, the machine was coming with me.

It took me a long time to get to the door that led into a hallway, and then came the task of opening the door. I had no strength and the door was incredibly heavy. I only had the use of my left arm. With a great struggle, I was able to wedge the machine into the crack I had managed to open in the door. After that, it was easy to get through the door.

I leaned on the machine and made my way down a lighted hallway. As I passed a glass display case, I saw an apparition. It was a Boris-Karloff-like specter of something vaguely human. Its color was purple-gray. One arm stuck straight out to the side and there was huge white lump below the protruding arm. It was puffy, like a soft balloon, and just as fragile. Shocks of long red hair raced akimbo around a dreadful face. The look of death. *Oh Jesus, God help me, that creature in the glass is me.*

I heard voices in the distance. I was determined to find someone, anyone who could help me. My rolling escort and I made it to a bend of the hallway. We made the turn and continued toward the voices. A group of six nurses was sitting at a table eating pizza. One of them looked up at me and leaped to her feet. Then, like marionettes tousled by the puppeteer, they each sprung from their chairs and turned toward me.

Two of them burst into tears. One began to scream and another covered her mouth with her hand. The last one stood facing me with her arms outstretched, hands raised as in a stopping motion. "What? What in God's name? What do you want?" In that second I realized—to them, I was a ghost, a harbinger ... a visitor from another world.

With my fingers still gripping the rolling machine, I motioned to the nurse who spoke to me to come closer. She somehow understood my pitiful gesture. She slowly came closer. I could only whisper.

"I want a bed ... I want my hair combed ... and a T.V." She hesitated, just for a moment, and then shot a quick glance down the hallway from where I had turned the corner. The sign on the wall read "To the Morgue."

In seconds, one of the nurses left and came back with a gurney. They detached me from the machine and wheeled me into a patient room. Someone lifted me onto the bed. They began wrapping me from the feet up. One explained that they were putting "anti-embolism" cloth on me. I was dressed in a fresh gown and covered with a blanket. I asked what time and day it was.

A nurse looked at her watch and said, "It's a quarter 'til two in the morning. Thursday morning." *Thursday morning?* I remembered that I had gone into surgery on Tuesday morning. I had *died* and the Lord had sent me back. Had I really been gone that long? No wonder they were frightened. I would have been frightened too.

The warmth of the blanket helped me drift off to sleep. They had already given me an I.V., along with an injection for pain. The pain was unendurable—a fight for my life. A large tube ran from my side to a machine next to me.

After many hours, I awoke thinking about what might have happened. It was the warlock's curse. I was sure of it. It had worked; the curse had worked, but only for a little while. The Lord had been looking after me. He had sent me back. I could not understand at the time, why He had decided to bring me back into this life. However, He had and that was good enough for me.

As I lay there, a nurse came into the room to check on me. "Do you need anything? She asked.

I whispered, "If you could turn on the television that would be great. Thank you."

A breaking news bulletin glared from the screen: "President Ronald Reagan has been shot during an assassination attempt." They shot Reagan on Monday. He was still alive and so was I. Strange. How much can happen in the course of one day.

The next day I seemed to flow in and out of consciousness. My room was on the bottom floor and I could see it was dark outside. As I gazed at the distant lights through the window of my room, a night nurse came in. She said "hello" and sat down beside the bed. "When you are able, you should call your mother. We found her phone number listed as your emergency contact. She was told to "make arrangements" for you. Do you understand what I mean? They told her that you had passed ... and now ... you are alive. You should call her as soon as you can." I nodded. I appreciated her kindness.

The next morning, I called my mother, collect. "Hello," I heard my mother say. "Will you accept the charges the operator asked my mother, "from Micky?"

"Is this some kind of a joke?" Mother screamed into the phone.

"No madam, this is the operator. Will you accept the charges?"

"It's me ... Mom," I whispered behind the operator's voice. "Mom can you hear me?"

"Yes, yes operator, I will accept the charges. Oh my God, can this be true. Micky … is that you? Are you … are you okay?"

"Mom, don't pay any attention to what they tell you, I'm still here."

"Okay, kid." I could hear her crying as I hung up the phone. I was exhausted and drifted off to sleep.

***

It was Sunday afternoon. After lunch, some of the nurses came by my room. Most of them were carrying large floral arrangements—there were eleven in all. Beautiful things. Baskets of carnations, white lilly's in planted pots, red and yellow roses. The room smelled like a floral shop. At one point in the afternoon, a nurse came in and opened one of the screened-bottom windows across from me. I could sense the air outside, but I was not strong enough to take advantage of a light breeze. I motioned for the nurse and she bent down to listen to my whisper. "Where are all the flowers coming from … who is sending me flowers?" I asked.

"Let's find out, shall we?" She began pulling the acknowledgment cards from each vase and gave them to me in a neat stack. "Here you go, sweetie."

Each one carried the name of a different church. Eleven in all. I knew that I had never been to any of them. How do they know I am in the hospital? I wondered. Although it was a mystery, it was a pleasant one. I decided to enjoy this blessing. God was looking after me. How beautiful. All afternoon and into the night shift, the nurses would stop by to take a break and "smell the roses."

Night was coming. I was tired but not sleepy. As I lay in bed, I thought I heard someone call my name. "Micky, Micky … can you hear me?"

I looked in the direction of the open window. There in the moonlight stood a girl. Her face pressed against the screen. Her shoulder-length blonde hair was gently moving in the breeze. I recognized her. It was Monica. I worked with her at the pharmacy. "Micky, can you hear me?" She repeated softly.

I looked at her and nodded. "Yes, Monica, I can hear you. What are you doing here?"

"Micky, you're not going to believe this, but they put your obituary in the newspaper."

"You need to get out of here." Then she was gone as quickly as she had come. I wondered why she had not come into my room to tell me that news. Why stand outside and try to speak with someone in the hospital through an open window? I thought about what she had told me. *My obituary was in the paper.* I wondered.

When I awoke, I stared at the large tube, which ran from my right side to the machine beside my bed. It reminded me of R2-D2 from the "Star Wars" movie. I had seen it as a new release the previous summer. My sense of humor was coming back.

The following morning, I woke up early. At around 9:00 the surgeon, who had also been my emergency room doctor, came to check on me and see how I was healing. He looked greatly stressed.

"Hi Micky, I'm Dr. Hattel. Do you remember me from the emergency room or after your operation?"

"Yes, I remember you quite well. Is something wrong?" He began to cry. The tears streaked down his face. This was a new experience for me. I had never seen a doctor cry.

"I want you to know, I am sorry … so sorry about the pain you felt during the operation to repair your lung. You felt the entire incision. You were screaming. I will never forget it as long as I live. You are too young to have to go through this procedure and endure that level of pain. I am sorry. Your wounds were so severe. I really have never seen anything like it." He wiped his eyes again, and left the room. I did not have the strength to cry. It made sense to me that they did not understand my wounds. They were from a supernatural source.

The Warlock understood the extent of my wounds. He understood because he was the one who had caused them. I wanted to go home. I missed my home, my dog, my job, and my friends. Most of all, I missed my mother. I knew I had to be strong. There was no one here for me. I clung to my faith and the knowledge that whatever else I faced next from this evil man, I would never have to face it alone. One thing was obvious to me. My faith in God had saved me from a premature death. I remembered a verse I had read years ago from the Bible: "my enemies will come at me one way, but they will flee seven ways." I clung to that verse and my faith. That kept me going on.

Days flowed in and out. In one of my lucid moments, I asked a nurse if I could have my purse. I was not sure if it was with me in my hospital room. I remembered hearing that my neighbor had brought my purse to the hospital.

The nurse promised me she would check around. She did not seem to know where it might be. She excused herself, and left my room, promising that she would find out about the purse and let me know something as soon as she could.

A few hours later she came back into my room—purse in hand. "I found this in the ER, I don't know why it didn't come with you to your room, but it didn't." The purse gave me comfort. It was something from home.

Two more days rolled by. My system was slowly detoxing. I felt much better, but the pain was unshakable. It was hard, and relentless. It never really went away completely. The pain meds could never give the pain the "knock-out" punch that I needed. It was a "technical knock-out."

On Friday, I had two visitors. It was Jeff and his wife Pat. What a pleasure it was to see a familiar face. I was thrilled. I wondered how they knew I was in the hospital.

"Hi Micky, how are you feeling? I am so sorry this happened to you," Pat told me. It was weird, she would talk to me but she would never look at me. She kept covering her eyes with her hands or burying her face into Jeff's chest. At least Jeff looked at my face. I had not seen myself in a mirror so I was not sure how bad it was. I knew that I must look terrible. My trusty R2-D2 stood beside me, along with my IV stand, which was loaded down with bags of fluids. At least I was not purple. Not anymore.

"Micky, I went by your house to get your dog." Jeff said. She is a sweet dog. We took her home to our house. It is no trouble. We took the dog food you had in the kitchen and she seems content ... but she misses you."

"Thank you both so much for doing that. I know Butchie is glad that you came to get her."

As we talked, I would periodically cringe with pain. It swept over me, like birth pains—slow at first but then more and more intense. I did not want to scare Pat away, but the rolling pain was too much to hide. They stayed a few minutes and then made their excuses and left. I was tired, even from such a short visit, but I was grateful to see someone I knew. A pleasant nurse came in to check my IV. She checked the tube in my side and then she took my temperature and blood pressure. She actually smiled and asked me how I was doing. I smiled back.

"Is it okay if I try to stand ... maybe sit in a chair?"

"Sure," the nurse told me. "Let's give it a try and see how you do."

I tried to stand, but I was still too weak. She helped me to lay my head back on the pillows, and told me, "We'll try again tomorrow. You'll be stronger tomorrow, and every day after." She patted my arm, which gave me hope. I wanted to fight. The Warlock was not going to win. Not this time.

The next day when the same nurse came in, she took my vitals and then asked me if I was ready to "try again." "Do you want to try and stand?"

"Oh, yes." She went to the doorway and looked down the hall.

She glanced back at me and said, "Okay, let's try it."

She helped me into a seated position on the side of the bed. I was looking at R2-D2. He had nothing to say, which did not surprise me. "Okay," she told me. "So far we are doing really well. Let us see if you can hold your own weight for just a moment. —Ready ... now." With that, she lifted me to my feet. I only lasted a few seconds but I was standing and holding my own weight. I was so grateful.

"Wow you did great!"

I looked at her with a smile and said, "Alright, let's try again tomorrow." She laughed and winked at me with thumbs up. I felt great—*maybe I am going to make it out of here.*

The next few days continued with the same routine. On Sunday, a couple came into my room that I did not recognize. They had kind eyes and pleasant smiles. The man introduced himself. "My name is Chuck and this is my wife Erma. We are friends of your friend, Jeff."

"Hello, thanks for coming."

"Jeff told us about your situation. Our son is a cancer survivor. He was in this hospital for treatment. My wife and I have spoken with Jeff and with the nurses here. The staff says you should be able to come home in a few days, 'if you have someone who can stay with you.'

We are here to offer to take you home with us when the hospital releases you. My wife will take good care of you." Tears rolled down my face. I could not thank them enough. They told me that they lived a few blocks from Pat and Jeff. They smiled as they left and said they would come back for me in a few days. I could not thank God enough. I knew he was looking after me. I was actually going to get out of here. Very soon.

The next morning, a new doctor I had not seen before told me he was going to remove the tube from my side. "If you do well for the next twenty-four hours, you will be able to go home. Do you have someone you can stay with for a while?"

"Oh, yes," I said, "I have some friends that I will be staying with." After removing the large tube in my side, I watched him leave the room rolling away R2-D2. I would not miss him.

The following morning a nurse removed the IV from my arm. "I understand you are being released today. I'll bet you're happy about that." I smiled and nodded.

A few hours later Erma came into the room carrying a large paper bag. "Are you ready to leave this joint?" she asked. Boy was I ever. She pulled a large bathrobe and a pair of slippers from the bag and helped me get dressed. It was not long before my surgeon came in to give me instructions about post-operative treatment.

"Micky," he said, "You will be in a lot of pain for quite some time. You need to stay ahead of the pain. Take your pain medications on a regular schedule, every four hours. You will also need to drink a liquid codeine every four hours in between the pills. I have scheduled you an appointment at my office in ten days. Good luck."

"Thank you, doctor. I appreciate all you have done for me."

He handed the prescriptions to Erma. He placed his hand on my shoulder as he said again, "Good luck. I'll see you in a few days." A nurse came in and helped me into a wheelchair. It was finally time to go.

The sun was shining outside. As Erma stepped into the car she said, "I know today will be hard for you. I know you are in a lot of pain, but I need to stop at the drug store and get these prescriptions filled."

Erma stopped at the drugstore, where I had worked for the last five years. I was scared to death. I had no idea what they would think. I looked awful. My hair needed washing, no makeup, and still in my bathrobe. This was not going to be good.

"I'll have to bring you in with me because I don't know how long it will take to fill the prescriptions," Erma said. "I can't leave you here in the car alone."

Great, I thought to myself. They will all gather around and want to know how I am doing. What a nightmare.

It was a real comedy and a struggle to get me out of the car. I had to lean on Erma to be able to walk. My right side was immobile. No weight on my right side. Left side only.

Slowly we made our way to the front door. She sat me down in one of the booths in front of the soda fountain. I could feel the stares. I looked up at some of the faces I knew well. The girls that I had worked with and laughed with for so long just stood in silence and stared with expressions of fear on their faces. A customer I knew walked by and I said, "Oh … hi."

Fear crossed her face. She literally turned and cut back up the aisle the way she came. I thought about how Monica had come to the window of my hospital room. I was like a Frankenstein monster.

God knows I looked like the walking dead. They had all had time to hear the gossip about what had happened to me. I realized they were looking at me with fear and superstition. Something that no longer belonged, a ghost. Erma helped me and we slowly made our way to the door.

A second customer, a middle-aged truck driver, a regular named Don, held the door open for us. The same reaction was on his face, recognition, fear and silence. I could feel the stares as Erma helped me back into her car. When we reached her home, she led me into a bedroom. She said it had been her son's room. After a little soup and medication, I was out like a light. It had been a hard day in so many ways. Chuck and Erma's kindness knew no bounds.

Each evening Erma would help me to the kitchen table for dinner. Chuck always said grace. I thanked the Lord constantly for both of them. Two weeks rolled by and I began to walk on my own. I still could not use my right arm. Sometimes it felt like it had no skin on it. Especially if the painkillers were wearing-off.

At the end of the third week, the plan was to move me into Pat and Jeff's house. I finally got to see Butchie, my Australian Blue Dingo and my best friend. She did a back flip when she saw me. She whimpered as I clutched her head with my left hand. My faithful friend.

The next day Pat drove me to my house in Delta to get some of my clothes. When we pulled into the driveway, I realized my car was gone. Where is my car, I wondered. I was too tired to worry about it.

***

A few weeks rolled by and I was gaining strength. Jeff and I were sitting at the kitchen table one morning having coffee. He seemed nervous. "Is something wrong, Jeff?" I asked.

"Mick, I hate to be the one to tell you this ... but the bank filed papers to repossess your house for nonpayment. But ... Mick, that's not all. Your car was stolen." The look in his eyes told me all I needed to know. We both knew who had taken my car. My ex-husband.

Pat eventually helped me to get a light job at the shop where she worked and soon after I was able to get my own apartment. Sadly, my beautiful little house was gone.

The warlock had not won the battle for my life, but he had won the war; my house and car were gone and my life was in complete disarray. At least for now ....

CHAPTER THIRTEEN

battle cries

Years later, I met a wonderful man who owned the house where I was living. He was kind and considerate and someone I grew to love. After some months of dating, we decided to get married. After we were married, we moved to Grand Junction, a much larger town not too far from Montrose. He owned a home there. It felt so good to be settled and away from the horrors of the warlock. I felt safe for the first time in a long time. I was in a new home, a new town, and I had a loving husband. Surely, I was out of the reach of Lee and his strangle hold.

We had been living in Grand Junction for about two years and life was good. I had not heard from Kathy for a while, but I always felt like if she needed me, she would find a way to contact me.

I had taken the day off work. I was sitting on the front porch. I saw the car as soon as it turned the corner. My brother Jimmy's old Buick pulled into our driveway. Riding beside him was my nephew. Christopher, Kathy's youngest son who was now sixteen. I was thrilled to see them both. I had not seen Jimmy or Chris for quite some time.

"Jimmy, you are the last person I expected to show up in my driveway. What's going on ... it's great to see you," I told him.

"Hi, Aunt Micky," Chris said as he gave me a warm hug. "I bet you didn't expect to see me or Uncle Jimmy did you?"

"No, but I am glad you are here."

I invited them in. Chris had several bags with him, so I suspected he was planning to stay for a while. That was okay with me. I better than most, understood how difficult it was to live with George Lutz. It was not hard to understand that Christopher needed to be out from under Lee's roof.

We all had dinner together that night. Jimmy left in the morning so he could get back to work and Chris stayed with me. He was a junior in high school so I did not waste any time getting him enrolled. I knew that Chris would need some guidance to find his way in the world. I decided that after he graduated high school, military service would do him some good.

Chris had not been with me for more than two weeks before I got a threatening phone call from Lee. I laughed at him as he hung-up the phone. It was too late. He had done all he could do to me. Now he was powerless … at least that is what I hoped and prayed for, that Lee would be powerless to hurt Chris or me.

I could not quite shake the feeling of being once again, in a spiritual battle.

Kathy had borne two more children since she and Lee had married. Two girls. Mom kept me well informed on what was going on with Kathy, Lee, and the kids. Mom had told me that Lee and Kathy had moved out of her house about a week after I left for Texas.

After I left home, I almost never spoke to Kathy. I kept up with her and the kids through conversations with Mom. Lee never wanted Kathy to be close to me. He felt threatened by our relationship and he wanted to make sure that Kathy was isolated. Kathy would only talk to Mom on the phone. I was always hopeful that she would call me one day. Now Chris was living with me, I hoped she would call to check up on him. Chris seemed to be adjusting well. He was back in school and making a few friends. He still had fear of Lee. At night, he insisted on sleeping with a knife under his pillow.

As time passed, Kathy began to call me every now and then. At first, we would only talk for two or three minutes. However, over a period of weeks, she began calling more and I had the sense that Lee was not home as much.

Kathy's marriage to Lee was falling apart. According to her, he was "sleeping around" with other women. Based on what I knew of Lee, I believed her. When we talked, her voice was always sad and filled with stress. She was desperately unhappy and I always got the sense that she was constantly looking over her shoulder, hiding her feelings. She seemed to be afraid all the time. I wondered how she had endured it—she had been married to Lee for nearly ten years. When I asked why she stayed with him, she always said it was "for the children." Based on what I had learned and seen from Chris, the children were miserable and scared, just like their mother. I think she did not know how to get away from him. He had taken control of her family, her time, her ability to see friends or to go out—he had even taken control of her thoughts. I do not think she could imagine her life without his control.

Months Later

My brother Jimmy pulled into my driveway again. This time he had his two young children with him.

"Mick, I'm sorry to drop this on you. You don't have to do this, but Carrie is leaving me. She wants the kids, but everything is so unsettled right now. I want them to stay with you so they don't have to hear all the fighting. We are losing the house, and I need a safe place for Jim Jr. and Katie to stay. Mick, will you help me out?"

"Of course they can stay here! We could enroll them into the local elementary school tomorrow."

"Thank you, Micky. This means everything to me. I don't know when Carrie is going to get her head on straight again. I think she has a lover, but I'm not sure. She has filed for divorce and we have to wait to see what the judge has to say about where the kids stay."

Suddenly, my husband James and I had three kids in our house. Our home became bustling and busy. My husband was a mail carrier and I managed a liquor store his parents owned. I worked every weekday, but the weekends were just for family. We did fun things like going fishing, taking in an occasional movie, or spending a peaceful day at home watching television. As Jimmy's divorce moved into the final stages, he received a court order to bring the children back to New York. Even though they had only gotten to stay a few months, I was heartbroken to see them leave. They had really settled in and loved the new school. My husband and I had taken to the new bustling household and I knew we would both miss them terribly. As all of this was happening, the Warlock's spiritual attacks began to increase.

***

I had an odd feeling when I awoke that morning. Chris was going out and spending the night at his best friend's house. My husband was going to work and I was looking forward to spending some much-needed time alone. Although I was feeling fine, I had a sensation of dread. It felt as though black clouds were gathering around me and a storm was coming. My thoughts took me back to that old fairy tale: "something wicked …this way comes." Something was not right and I knew where the feelings came from.

Over the years, I had come to recognize when Lee had placed a spell or a curse on me.

In my spirit, I had a deep sense of *knowing*. The knowing told me that evil was coming. I knew he was behind it. I sat on my living room couch for a time, thinking about the Warlock, my sister, and her children—I began to pray.

I had been praying for some minutes when a sudden, loud banging noise came from the kitchen. I finished my prayer and walked into the kitchen. Dozens of little sparrows were flying against the large kitchen window. Repeatedly, they slammed against the window. I stood motionless and watched in amazement. They were trying to *warn me*—something was coming. It was coming for me. I was overwhelmed with gratitude for these small creatures who had given me warning. Many Christians have also received early warnings of impending danger from birds.

As soon as I spoke the words "Thank you," the sparrows stopped as suddenly as they had started. I stood in silence. Something is coming, I thought to myself, but I cannot hide from it. I kept muttering the words I had learned so many years ago from the Bible: "He has given His angels charge over thee and they shall keep thee in all thy ways. They will lift thee up with their hands, lest ye dash thy foot against a stone."

I felt a tremendous sense of comfort in recalling that verse. Something was coming, but I would not have to fight it alone. I decided to go about my day and make it as productive and happy as I could, under the circumstances.

I knew that I had many hours of laundry to attend too. In the laundry room I began sorting clothes and preparing them for the washing machine. As I worked, my sense of dread increased. Still, the afternoon passed without incident. Around five in the afternoon, my husband came home from work.

When James walked in the front door, he stopped at the threshold and looked at me. "What is it, Mick? Something is wrong; I can see it in your face."

"I'm not sure how to tell you this, but … I think …. I know … something very evil is coming to our house—tonight." A look of fear and amazement covered his face.

"Mick does this have anything to do with your sister's husband?"

"I am afraid it has everything to do with Lee"

"I don't know what to do! What can I do to help you?" His eyes searched my face for an answer. He had experienced more than once the odd occurrences and the strange phone calls. He knew that when that feeling came over me, something was going to happen.

"Don't worry about it, James," I told him. "Don't worry about it. The Lord is in charge here and I'll take care of it."

"Mick, I know you are right," James said. "I just hope you know what you are doing. I do not want you to get hurt. I don't want any of us to get hurt." He relaxed a little as we sat down at the table to have our dinner. Although I knew that my husband would do anything, including risking his life to protect me, I was on my own. Not knowing what more we could say, we went into the living room and turned on the television. We sat on the couch together for a couple of hours but we did not talk. It was as if a silent cloud had descended over the house. I knew that now was the time for me to marshal my concentration, and call in the angels for protection.

Around 10 p.m., James said, "Mick, I don't understand why I'm so tired. I feel like my eyes are closing shut without any help from me. I do not want to leave you here alone, but I have to go to sleep. Are you going to be okay if lay down in the bedroom?"

"It's okay … I will be alright. If I need you I will holler, I promise." I walked with him into the bedroom and kissed him goodnight. He was sound asleep in moments. I knew that I could not allow myself to sleep. I knew I had to stay awake … I had to face this thing. Now. Tonight. I waited. I just did not know for what.

After several minutes, our three dogs in the backyard began whimpering and banging their bodies against the back door. They always did that when they wanted in, but there was never howling. *Why are they whimpering?* I walked into the laundry room to open the back door. All three dogs poured into the room. The oldest, a large golden lab immediately stuck her head in between the clothes dryer and the wall. Her body hit the floor with a thump. Butchie got underneath a wooden table and rolled herself into a ball with her paws over her face. The youngest dog ran to the corner of the room and stuck his face into the corner, then rolled himself into a ball. They were terrified. I had never before seen fear in my dogs. I whispered a quick prayer to the Lord for strength and sat down at the kitchen table. That is when it started. BANG! BANG! BANG! It sounded like something that weighed several hundred pounds was flinging itself against the side of the house.

The sound gravitated from the kitchen to the bedrooms, then the living room. I could not believe that my husband could sleep through the incredible noise.

The dogs did not move. Then IT entered the back wall of the laundry room. My feet stuck to the floor. I did not move. I felt that the Lord had warned me not to look it in the eyes. To do so would mean death.

The demon stood a few inches in front of me. I could feel its loathing. A stench filled the room that burned my nose and throat. It was big, several feet taller than I was. The room filled with its massive size and white-hot hate. I slowly raised my head so that I could see it from the chest down. I did not need to look into its face. I knew what it looked like and what it wanted—it wanted to kill me. No question. Pure wrath—an evil that hung on the air, and permeated the room. It shook as if in a rage, this demon from the pit of hell.

I spoke, "You have no business here! In the power of the name of the Lord Jesus Christ, get out of my house!"

I pointed my finger to the right. It took a step backward. I spoke again, "In the power of the name of the Lord Jesus Christ—I order you out of my house—NOW!"

IT seemed to hear my words and although the words infuriated this being, it obeyed the command. I felt the stifling, sickening breeze of its body turning away from me as it moved toward the living room. In the living room, it brushed against a potted, seven-foot tree. The tree reached nearly to the ceiling and the dirt inside the pot weighted over one-hundred pounds. As the demon passed through the living room wall it brushed against the tree leaving it cocked to one side; the pot ajar.

I was instantly aware of angels outside the kitchen wall. I heard the demon question an angel of the Lord.

"Why do I have to leave this house?" The specter from hell asked.

"Because she calls upon Jesus!" I heard the demon scream as if being dragged away a great distance. After the scream died away, the air rushed out of my lungs, and my legs trembled beneath me. I sat down on the couch, shaken and exhausted. It was over—at least for now. I got up and touched a branch of my tree. The branch and the leaves upon it, crumpled like ash in my hand. It was dead. I thanked the Lord for protecting us.

The dogs, who had not moved or uttered a sound during the entire ordeal, sat up and looked at me. "It's alright, it's alright," I said as I petted each one in turn. Incredibly, my husband still slept.

In the morning, James came into the kitchen and exclaimed, "Mick, what happened to the tree?"

I laughed as I said, "Do you really want to know?"

After that encounter, many strange incidents began to play out. I knew that this was just a skirmish, in the ongoing battle against Lee and his evil minions. I was being drawn into a war.

kathy moves on

Kathy called distraught. She was in tears. "Mick, it's over, it's all over. I'm scared Mick, and I don't know what to do."

"Tell me what's happened, Kathy."

"Oh, God … Micky, the house burned down. We lost everything."

"What happened? How did the house burn down?" I asked her.

"I'm not sure what happened, something about clothes catching on fire … it started in a closet. Lee has taken off to Las Vegas. The girls and I are stranded. My marriage is over, Mick."

I asked her what she wanted to do.

"I'm taking a job. There is a place not far from here, called the Village Pub. I'm going to waitress again."

"That sounds good Kathy, but where are you going to live? Have you found an apartment or a house for you and the girls? Do you need money?"

"Micky, you know I hate to ask, but yes, I need money to get us moved into an apartment. There is a two-bedroom apartment near my new job. It will be crowded with three girls, but I can get a sleeper sofa and we can make due. "

I told her I would send her $1,400 by overnight express. She gave me the address of the restaurant. She called the next day to tell me she had received the money. I was relieved; maybe she would be all right.

Kathy called me a week later. She said she had gotten an apartment for herself and the girls. The restaurant where she was working had taken up donations and she had all the beds and furniture she needed. Maybe she was getting stronger, coming out of her dependency and the controlled life she had led with Lee.

Two weeks later, I got another call from my sister. She sounded frightened. Lee had been in her apartment while she was gone; she was sure of it. "Why do you think he was in your apartment, Kathy?"

"He called me on the phone and described everything in my apartment. He was very threatening. I am so scared, Mick." I thought to myself that at least now, after getting some distance from Lee, she could finally admit to me what she had felt from almost the first day she started dating Lee—fear.

"Kath, don't let him scare you. You have a new life now, and Lee is not in it. Try not to let him intimidate you. Get the locks on the apartment changed so you have some peace of mind."

"You're right. He's just a bully, and I have let him bully me for too long." We hung up the phone, but Kathy and her situation was heavy on my heart. I knew what horrible things George Lee Lutz was capable of doing. I thought about the series of events that had led to her current situation:

> About a week after I left New York to meet Aaron in Texas, Mom told me that Kathy, George, and the kids had moved to California. Lee had purchased a nice home in a gated community using the proceeds from the Amityville contract.
>
> I was happy for Kathy and for the kids, but wondered if it would last. One afternoon, I got an unexpected call from Kathy. She was frantic.
>
> "Mick, he's going out with other women. I know he has been with other women in the past … but … this is too much. You won't believe what he did to me."
>
> "What happened Kathy, just calm down and tell me what happened."

Kathy is sobbing, but she manages to regain her composure and tell me what Lee has done.

"Mick, yesterday a woman and three children knocked on my front door. She said, 'I have an appointment with Lee, is he in?' Lee was in another room, so I told him that there was woman here to see him. He actually asked me to watch her kids while they *met* in our bedroom! For seven hours—. I *know* they had sex, Mick. I hate him, and I can't do this anymore."

I told her to calm down and to get hold of herself. "You know what he is capable of Kathy. Maybe it's time to do something different."

"I was so mad, that I told the woman's oldest child to watch her two siblings and I got in the van. I threw rocks from the driveway onto the bedroom window, and then drove around for an hour. When I came back home, the woman and her children were gone. It wasn't pretty, Mick, the argument we had was bad."

Several weeks after this phone call, Lee wound up losing the California house. According to Kathy, when the foreclosure was final, Lee had stripped the house. He took chandeliers, bathroom and light fixtures, anything he could remove. Kathy was so ashamed that she had a hard time telling me what he had done.

Sadly, she did not leave him … at least not then. The Lutz family wound up relocating to Phoenix, Arizona. Lee had talked his way out of losing his wife, and talked his way into another house. This house later burned down, according to Kathy, because of a mysterious fire that started in the closet.

I guess Lee was tired of taking care of his family. He left without a word, and wound up in Las Vegas. It was finally over.

Kathy and the kids, however, were abandoned and alone in Arizona with no money, no friends, and no one to help.

What a mess!

Several Weeks Later

Kathy called me and she was excited. She had met a woman who had agreed to let her make payments on a house that she was trying to sell. Kathy was going to own her own home. She was thrilled. The house was in Scottsdale. A beautiful house in a beautiful place. My sister sounded great for the first time in a very long time. Things were going much better for her. I was convinced that living in Arizona and finding a beautiful home meant Kathy's luck was changing. We could not see the future, but the rarified air of Scottsdale, Arizona would hold new dangers for Kathy. Dangers that we could not have imagined at the time.

Kathy had not heard from Lee since she had changed the locks. Her biggest problem was that the car had died and she needed a new car.

After we hung up, I could not stop thinking about Kathy trying to care for the three girls and herself, with no car. Danny, Kathy's oldest son, had long-ago moved out and Chris was still living with me. It was Friday morning and I went to a local car dealership. I bargained the owner to his bottom-dollar price on a butter-cream colored, Ford LTD. The kind of car I knew Kathy would like. Big and powerful.

I took the car home and parked it in my driveway. Their mechanic had told me that it would be a good idea to change the thermostat in Arizona because of the change in elevation. Other than that, I was "good to go."

When my husband and Christopher came home, I told them what I had in mind. This was going to be a big surprise. I wanted to drive the car down to Arizona over the weekend and surprise Kathy. They both liked the idea and we planned to make a road trip over the weekend.

Saturday morning, we got up early and Chris, James, and I left for Arizona. I had purchased a roll of red-crepe paper to use later on. When we pulled into the restaurant where Kathy worked, I parked the car at the empty end of the lot. I fastened two large crepe-paper bows on either side of the car. It looked great.

After decorating the car for the surprise, we walked inside the restaurant and sat at a table. Kathy was busy waiting on customers. When she came to our table, she stopped dead in her tracks. "What? What are you doing here?"

She hugged each of us. "I have a surprise for you when you can take a break," I told her. She was grinning and said, "Oh, great, I haven't had a nice surprise in a long time."

After she finished taking care of two customers, she came to our table and sat down beside me. "I have a few minutes now, Mick ... what's the big surprise?"

I told her we needed to go outside. As we walked out the front door, there was a pick-up truck and a van parked next to each other blocking the view of the end of the lot. We walked between them. I spun around and looked at her. "Give me your hand," I told her. I handed her some car keys, went to the end of the van, and pointed. "This is for you."

She came around the end of the van and looked. Her face was total astonishment. There was the car with big red bows. "I can't take this, Micky. You shouldn't have spent your money on a car for me."

"Oh, yes you can take it, and anyway, what's the money for if not for family? This is your car, now."

She undid one bow and sat in the driver's seat. My heart was in my throat. "Damn that's pretty," she whispered. We followed her back into the restaurant. Kathy was so excited she told everyone. What a wonderful day it was. We all flew home on Sunday evening.

The house she was now buying was big and beautiful. Kathy seemed settled in her job and the girls were happy.

I felt, at the time that things would be all right. I had only one reservation, she seemed a little weak to me, and she had a persistent cough. "What's going on with that cough? Kath? Are you okay?"

"Yeah, the doctor says it's from an allergy to a mold that is found in this part of the country. Something called *cocci*. I had never heard of it, but the doctor said it can be dangerous." Phoenix was one of four areas of the world where that strain of mold existed. According to the doctor, the mold had settled in her lungs.

As time went on, I realized that my sister was getting sicker by the day. As if that was not enough, she was fighting with Lee over the divorce. He was forcing her to sign all kinds of legal papers that she did not want to sign. In her weakened state, she just did not seem to have the strength to resist him.

One Friday, she called early in the afternoon. Her voice was shaky and she was scared to death. I kept trying to get her to tell me what was wrong, but she refused to talk about it over the phone. I knew she was afraid so I decided that I would fly down and surprise her.

It was late in the evening when I landed. After nine. I took a taxi to the restaurant. I stepped inside the front door. It was mostly dark so I knew that she was closing up. The place was quiet except for the soft sound of someone crying. It was Kathy.

She was praying. I heard her ask, "Lord, why can't you give me someone who will truly love me?"

"Excuse me." I said. She spun around. "I was just passing over with my parachute on, so I decided to drop in." She jumped up from her chair and squeezed the breath out of me.

Missy was in the back, washing dishes. She was just as surprised to see me. I stayed for the weekend, but I had to take an overnight flight back on Sunday so I could be at work on Monday. We had a great visit, but it was upsetting for me. Things were not good, the Warlock was on the rampage and Kathy was quickly succumbing to this mysterious illness.

I was not sure what I could do to help—spiritual forces had been unleashed against her—evil forces that emanated from the Warlock alongside the sickness brought on by the mold. .

combat zones

The phone rang. "Mick ... Mick!"

"What is it Kath?"

"He's coming, Mick—he's making me have lunch with him. He's going to make me sign more papers and I'm afraid. I don't want to go!"

"Slow down," I told her. "What do you mean a lunch ... what kind of 'papers?'"

"I am supposed to meet him at a restaurant. I know he is going to make me sign legal papers. He is trying to take away all my rights, Micky. What should I do? I don't want to go ... the truth is ... I'm afraid to go."

"Look, Kathy. Why don't I come with you? He won't bother you if I'm there."

"Can you do that? That would be great."

It was only a one-hour flight to Phoenix from my house. "Don't worry, I'll call you back and tell you what time to pick me up at the airport tonight. Okay?"

When Kathy picked me up at the airport, she was shaken and worn-out. When we got to her house, she walked in the door and plopped down on the couch, her hands covering her face. She began to sob. I let her cry. I think it was more from relief than sadness. She had been carrying this burden and dealing with her abject fear of Lutz for a long time ... too long.

"I can't tell you how much better I feel knowing that you are coming with me. Sorry for all the waterworks, but I have needed to that for a long time."

"Kathy, listen to me. He is not going to make you sign anything tomorrow—nothing. I promise. I won't let him get away with it."

She stood up and hugged me. "Okay, Mick ... I can do this thing if you are with me."

"How about I make us a cup of tea and then we'll get some sleep." When I came back from the kitchen, Kathy was still on the couch, but slumped forward. Her elbows resting on her knees. She stared straight ahead, a million miles away.

"Come on, here is your tea. Drink it and let's get some sleep."

"I'm afraid of him, Mick. I always have been. Even when we dated, I knew that there was something wrong with him. I could not understand it then, in the early days. All I focused on was how nice he was to me. Yet, in the back of mind, I think I knew that he would hurt me … hurt all of us in the end."

"I know. However, you have to think of yourself and the kids now. He has controlled you from the very beginning, but now it is time to take back that control. You will be okay, Kathy … tomorrow and *after* tomorrow. You will break the power he has over you."

We drank the tea in silence and went to bed. I could hear her softly crying in her bedroom. I prayed that tomorrow would go well for her and that Lutz's hold would diminish.

Kathy was not the only one having a tough time sleeping. I tossed and turned most of the night. Always thinking about the Warlock. Lutz had no idea that I would be with her tomorrow. What will it be like for him to have someone walk into a room that he tried to murder? My sister knew nothing about the curse I had received in the mail. She knew nothing about my visit from one of his demons. I did not want her to know. She was already frightened enough; why make things worse for her?

The next day, we were getting ready for our ominous lunch with Lee and my sister walked into the bathroom. I was getting dressed and she saw my scar.

"Oh, my God, Micky …what happened? That looks horrible."

"It's a long story. Let's just say it is a token reminder of a bad patch."

Kathy never asked me another question about the scar. The look on her face told me that she suspected that it might have something to do with her soon-to-be ex-husband. People, damaged by an evil person, often have a decided lack of curiosity concerning the trials and tribulations of others. They can barely handle their own hurts and fears, and they just cannot take on anyone else's pain. Because of that, my "bad patch" explanation was enough for her. She did not know what had happened to me and I did not want her to know. The same self-preservation mechanism had shut her down all those years she had been married to Lee. It was easier to pretend not to notice than to face the terrible truth that the person you are married to is evil.

I silently prayed for both of us as we drove to our meeting. Kathy's hands were trembling. It took ten minutes to get to the restaurant. It was nice enough place. Not too many people inside from the looks of the parking lot. It was 11:30, a little early for the full lunch crowd. Lee had parked his late-model luxury car near the front door.

"He must already be inside," Kathy said as we walked in the front door. She was shaking like a leaf. I took her arm in mine and she leaned on me ever so slightly. It was as if she wanted to be brave but the fear of what she was about to face was beginning to overwhelm her.

He was standing just inside the front door. Dressed in a sweater and a pair of dress pants, he looked like he had aged significantly. I caught the look in his eyes as he saw me. Astonishment and anger. It had been many years since he had seen me and this was not going to be a happy reunion. I wondered what it would be like to have someone that you had murdered step into a room with you and say "hello." If he was rattled, he was trying his best not to show it.

He turned to me, and with eyes as dead as the grave, he pointed and said, "This way. I have a table in the corner. Somewhere we can be alone and talk."

He led us to a table at the far end of the restaurant, in the corner of the large room. I didn't' want to think about why he had chosen such a hidden table, but it was Lee, and he always had an agenda. A hidden one.

I knew my presence angered him. He did not try to hide his chagrin. Lee was never one to let his feelings languish on the inside. He jerked a chair away from the table. "Sit," he barked at Kathy. She instantly obeyed—trained and expected to do Lee's biding instantly and without question.

He pointed to a chair across from Kathy. I supposed that was his way of telling me where to sit. I ignored his gesture and seated myself directly across from him. I needed to be able to see his eyes and to watch him closely.

A waitress approached our table. "May I take your order? I ordered a coffee and a water. Kathy did the same. Lee was annoyed.

"Well I guess we're not eating," he said as he looked at me with a scowl. He ordered a coffee. The waitress returned in minutes with our drinks.

Lee turned his attention towards Kathy. He placed his arm around the back of her chair and leaned into her,

I watched as Kathy began to sink physically in her chair. Her arms dropping limp to her sides. A scenario that I had seen playout so many times before. I knew what he was doing. He was not speaking. He was using his mind-control on her. I felt the Lord's hand on me, and by some miracle, I could hear in my head, the thoughts that emanated from Lee's mind. *Suddenly I knew I had the gift.*

Without speaking, I screamed at him, *Heeeeey ... hey!* Lee spun around and looked at me in disbelief. I then said to his mind, *If you say one more word to Kathy, just one more word—. Do you see that knife on the table between us?* His eyes fell immediately to the knife. I thought to him, *If you say one more syllable I am going to stick that knife through your larynx ... right here ... right now.*

Lee braced himself as if struck. Sweat drops formed on his face. Now he was sinking physically in *his* chair, a look of fear in his eyes. He stared at me, then sprang from his chair, and ran to the men's room. I glanced at my watch, and leaned over to bring Kathy out of her trance.

"Kathy wake up ... you have to snap out of it, now."

As though waking from a long nap, Kathy sat up and said, "What's happened, Mick?"

"This lunch is over. Try and sip some of your coffee because we need to go ... soon."

"But, where's Lee?" she said.

"He's in the men's room." I said. "We're leaving as soon as he comes back. I would leave now but I don't think we should give him the impression that we are afraid." It took twenty-three minutes for Lee to return to the table. Without a word, he snatched the check the waitress had left, grabbed his briefcase, (which he had underneath the table) and walked away. We watched as he sped away in his car.

During the trip home, I silently thanked the Lord for protecting us. I flew home the following morning. Kathy seemed relieved and I hoped it would last.

What had happened in the restaurant reminded me of the story in Exodus, when Moses stood before the Pharaoh to convince him to release the Jewish people who had worked as slaves serving the Egyptians. Over the course of several weeks, Moses and his brother Aaron sought an audience with the Egyptian king. Repeatedly, Moses asked the king to "let my people go." The king steadfastly refused. Exasperated, Moses told Aaron, his brother, to release his staff and throw it on the ground. Aaron did as Moses had requested, and the staff, when it hit the ground became a snake.

The Pharaoh, seeing the staff-turned-snake, spoke to his two sorcerers: "Do as he has done." The sorcerers, being clever at their craft, were able to turn their two rods into two snakes. However, the snake created by Moses' staff devoured the two snakes conjured by the weak magic of the king's sorcerers. God will not be mocked. This day, God had mocked the Warlock's powers. I just happened to have been the one that God used to accomplish His end. The Warlock had not been in charge that day. He had been humbled.

I wondered what would be next. I would not have to wonder long.

The weeks rolled quietly by with no word from Kathy. Then one morning I got another frantic call. I could hear the panic in her voice. "Mick, he's coming here … I mean … here, to my house!"

"When? When is he coming?"

"Tonight, Mick."

I glanced at my clock and said, "Kath, let me call you back in a few minutes." I called the airline and booked myself on the next flight. I called my sister back and told her what time I would meet her at her house.

I barely made the flight on time. As I sat in my assigned seat on the plane, I said under my breath, "Here we go again." *What is he up to now? I wish he would just leave her alone.*

When I arrived at her house, she was in a complete panic. "Mick, I don't want that *spirit* in my house." She began to cry.

"What time is he supposed to come?" She glanced at the clock in the kitchen.

"In two hours," she said.

"We need to go to the grocery store, right now," I told her. She looked at me with a puzzled expression. "Trust me. We have to hurry."

We jumped into the car and sped off. Kathy stayed in the car while I went in the grocery store. I quickly found the baking aisle and selected a bottle of extra virgin olive oil. As she drove us home, she asked me, "Mick what are we doing? Why did you buy that stuff?"

"I'll show you when we get home," I told her.

During the ride home, I prayed for the Lord to anoint the olive oil. Without his hand, we would be helpless. I felt the Lord touch the oil as I held it in my arms. Once inside the house, I explained, "We are going to seal the door."

"What do you mean ... 'seal the door?'"

I opened the front door as far as it would go. Kathy stood and stared at me, fascinated. I coated my fingertips with oil and spread it across the outside door-jam. I spread it twice across the bottom of the doorway and said, "In the name of Jesus." I covered the doorframe with the anointed oil. Finished, I closed the door and waited for Lee to arrive. Kathy was bewildered. She asked, "What does it mean ... the oil on the door? Why are you doing that?"

"Don't worry, you'll see." It was not long before we heard a car pull into the driveway. She looked out the window. "It's Lee ... he's here."

I told her not to be frightened and not to tell him that I was here. "When he knocks on the door, don't be afraid, open the door as far as it will go. I'll be hiding behind it."

I stood against the wall, waiting. "Go ahead Kath, don't worry," I whispered.

We heard the knock. Kathy was shaking. I nodded for her to open the door.

She opened it as far as it would go. Lee climbed the three steps to the front door, and said, "I have some things for you to sign ... whether you like it or not." He tried to step through the doorway but could not pass the threshold. Kathy stepped back. Her face was a mask of fear and confusion. Lee cursed as he struggled to pass through the doorway. In a rage, he pounded his fists against the door jam. I wanted to laugh. The warlock had once again, been thwarted. Lee screamed at Kathy, "Fuck it," he said and turned. I listened to his heavy footsteps retreating to his car. Lee wasted no time in speeding away.

Kathy slammed the door shut. With her arms extended high above her head, she spun around and landed on the couch, her arms still in the air. I set the bottle of oil on the table between us. "Mick ... that was the best use of olive oil I have ever seen. What just happened?" She was laughing. It had been a very long time since I had seen my sister laugh and it felt good.

I laughed, too. "You said you didn't want that *spirit* in your house!" She jolted into a sitting position and stared at me.

"But how? How did you do that?"

"Kath, the Lord sealed the doorway with the blessed oil—it's that simple. There's no way Lee could cross over it."

She shook her head and looked at me. "Did that really just happen? Awesome." She was grinning a wide, satisfied grin.

She shook her head again. Then she pointed at the bottle of oil. "What are we going to do with that?"

"Well, I think it might be a good idea to put it away and save it for next time. You might need it again." She picked up the bottle and hid it in her bedroom. "What do we do now?" She asked when she came back.

"Don't worry. He is not coming back tonight. I think Lee is probably quite confused. Let's have a cup of tea to celebrate."

I tried to speak about old things and make her laugh. In the back of my mind, I kept thinking about how once again the Lord had humbled the Warlock.

One week later, Kathy called me again. She was very upset. Lee had called and told her that he would leave some papers for her to sign in her mailbox. His instructors were to "sign the papers and put them back in the mailbox in *one* hour."

Kathy asked me, "Mick, what should I do?"

"Kathy … you still have the bottle of blessed oil. It is a weapon. Use it!"

"But, Mick, how do I use it? What should I do?"

"Go and get the oil," I said, "Go to the mailbox and I will walk you through what you should do." Her mailbox was an old-fashioned box with a pull-down flap in the front. I told her to rub the oil completely over the opening of the mailbox. "That's all you have to do, Kathy. Just watch what happens when Lee comes to drop-off the papers."

We hung up the phone. After an hour had passed, Kathy called me back. "Mick, I watched Lee through the blinds in the living room. He could not open the mailbox. He got mad and punched it, then got in his car and left," she told me as she laughed hysterically. I laughed too. We laughed together as we hung up the phone.

I thought to myself, *the warlock was humbled by a mailbox.* The Lord uses simple things to confound the wise."

fatalities

Several months passed, and although I spoke with my sister infrequently, we had seemingly solved the "Lee" question. In spite of that, Kathy was not doing well. Her immune system compromised, she was having trouble fighting off recurring lung infections. She often had chills and fever, and difficulty breathing which sometimes required short stays in the hospital. Hospital visits became much more frequent and the length of each stay grew longer.

My sister was slowly fading to the cocci-mold disease. She was disappearing. Kathy had never been heavy, but now she was painfully thin and weak. Still, she was a fighter. I was lucky enough to go with her to one of her appointments to see her primary doctor, Doctor Ruben.

As she went through tests, he brought me into his office to talk to me about her condition. Dr. Ruben was world renown in the field of immunology and his specialty was fungal infections. He had received a federal grant in the US to do a medical trial. He had twenty-five subjects that he could admit to the trial. Kathy was number twenty-five. I listened intently as he explained to me the four parts of the world where this mold existed. He pointed to a world map on the wall of his office and began to explain what was wrong with my sister:

"Your sister has what is sometimes called 'Valley Fever.' Valley Fever was discovered in the San Joaquin Valley of California. Some people call it 'desert rheumatism.' Valley Fever is prevalent in the San Joaquin and Central Valleys of California, and in the hot, desert regions of southern Arizona—no doubt, where your sister was exposed. *Coccidiosis immitis* is also found in the soils of Central and South America

"People sometimes come into contact with the mold spores if they are around an excavation site. The spores live in the soil. If disturbed, the bacteria can be breathed into the lungs from the air.

"What your sister has is a 'sickness of degree.' Estimates vary, depending on the study, but roughly, sixty percent of the people who breathe the spores do not get sick. However, for some people, like Kathy, who is sensitive to this mold, it can be dangerous—even life threatening. Some people experience cold or flu symptoms, and some can become sick enough to develop pneumonia.

"Unfortunately, about one or slightly more, in two-hundred will develop the disseminated form, which can be devastating to a person's health … even in some cases … fatal.

"In Kathy's case, the disease has spread beyond the lungs, to the bloodstream, involving the skin, bones and membranes that surround the brain, causing meningitis, or brain swelling."

His goal was to develop a serum or serums to combat and defeat the toxic effects of the mold. As he spoke to me, I realized what he was really saying. There was no real hope for Kathy.

I felt grateful and privileged to have met and spoken with this man. He had done all that he could. I thanked him and shook his hand as I left his office. A nurse escorted me to a room where Kathy was waiting. They were just finishing their lab tests.

Ironically, in a short time I would be hospitalized myself for what they diagnosed to be "mold blood-poisoning." I spent three weeks in the hospital. It was not cocci.

Kathy was terrified that since I had spent so much time in Phoenix that I would get sick too. I told her it was not the same mold. The area of the country that I lived in had "black mold." For the next ten weeks, I would have to live on oxygen and confined to my room. I knew exactly how Kathy felt. It would take me three months to recover. As soon as I was well enough to travel, I went to see Kathy.

She wondered why we both were so sensitive to mold. I would make her laugh cracking jokes about our Irish DNA. Tears were too overwhelming. We needed the laughter. She was on a breathing vent machine that sat next to her bed.

Summer 2004

I went to be with her for a week. We spent all of our time together in her room. We talked about old things. Each time she spoke of Lee, it was with terror and torment in her eyes. That bothered me. One afternoon Kathy began to cry. I said, "Kathy, what is it ... why are you crying?"

"Seb and I should never have broken up. It should never have happened," she said.

She was right and we both knew it. Seb had his faults, but he was a good person and he loved his children. He would never have done to Kathy what Lee had done. Never. We both sat crying with our hands pressed over our faces.

"You know," I told Kathy, "I'll never understand how we can have dry skin, dry eyes, and dry hair and yet we can cry fucking rivers."

That was the end of the tears. Kathy was laughing so hard she could hardly get her breath. "That was too damn funny," she told me.

"Yeah," I said, "truth hurts—doesn't it." We looked at each other and began laughing all over again. She soon fell asleep and I watched her. So many regrets.

At times when we talked, she would get off the vent and sit in a chair. She would cross her legs and speak with her hand in the air as she spoke of years past. During those moments, she was the "old Kathy" … the pistol of a girl. I loved so much. The doctors had told her she had three months to live. She never actually said that she was "terminal." She knew she was dying, but she had not said anything specific to the family. It is funny, if you have never seen anyone die, then you do not know what dying "looks" like. I remember how horrible I had looked when I woke up in the hospital. It was the most terrifying specter I had ever seen … me … wearing a mask of death. Somehow, seeing my sister, so shortly before her death, I was in complete denial. She is not dying, I thought. She has always been there. Surely, she will hang on for a long time. I refused to recognize that old bugaboo death, but he comes whether we recognize him or not. Had I realized her death was knocking at the door, I would have stayed. However, I did not, or would not see it. I left her to return home.

June 2004 -Kathy's Day

A few months before my sister Kathy's death, the family gathered to give to Kathy what we called a "living wake." Our plan was to spend the entire weekend with her: Mom, Aunt Nellie, Jimmy, Joan, me, and Kathy's children. A full weekend with her family is what she wanted. We were determined to give her that. She had been through so much. Kathy was 58; too young to be dying. It was ironic that she had survived all those years with evil all around her in the form of her ex-husband, Lee, and now, when she had finally broken free from his spell, she was being poisoned by a toxic mold. It was so unfair. We wanted this weekend to be a special time.

I arrived Thursday night, a day early. Kathy was still on oxygen but her eyes were bright. She was in her night-clothes.

We made tea and I sat with her on the couch. She was in a reflective mood, so I was quiet, hoping she might talk. She began to share her hopes of the weekend with me. "Mick, I want to be able to relax and enjoy having all of you around me. I do not want to think about the past, only this weekend—being with my family. Maybe we can read from the Bible, too."

She told me she had selected several passages from the Sermon on the Mount, from the Book of James, and one of her favorites from the Apostle Paul, in one of his letters to the church. "My strength is perfected in weakness," the apostle told us. In so many ways, Kathy had grown as a person after freeing herself from Lee. Her strength had been perfected. Her hope was that it would have a profound impact on all of us.

"Mick," she said, "... will you do me a favor? As I read from the Bible, will you study their faces? I want to make sure that they understand the deeper meaning. Watch each of them closely, Mick, and then after I am finished ... share their expressions with me."

"Sure, Kathy, I can do that." The following morning the rest of the family began arriving. There were lots of hugs and kisses all around. Some of the words were uplifting, but somber too.

We spent the rest of the day eating and talking. Lots of laughter, which I think helped everyone. I watched Kathy as she and Mom sat on the couch. I could see the tears in Mom's eyes, as she looked at her daughter. How can you tell your daughter how much you love her when you know that soon you will never be able to tell her again? Somehow, they got through the tough moments and managed to laugh.

Sunday morning, after breakfast, Kathy asked everyone to assemble in her living room. She sat on the large couch. Because she had lost so much weight, the couch seemed to swallow her frail body. She beamed as she scanned the faces gathered around her. Kathy began to read from the Bible. As she read, I remembered the promise I had made to my sister. "Study their faces," she had told me. I did, taking in each person's expression as I scanned the room.

After the reading, there was a silence in the room as each person contemplated what we must all face soon. We were losing Kathy.

She laid the Bible down beside her, and rested for a moment. After a few minutes, and with great effort, she rose from the couch. "I hope you will all understand, but I am so tired. I would like to go to my room and rest before lunch." As she slowly navigated the hallway to her bedroom, I quietly followed.

Once we were behind the closed bedroom door and she was settled in bed, she asked, "Well, Mick, what did you see? How did they look?"

I considered my answer carefully. "You did a wonderful job, Kathy. And you were right; your words had a great impact on everyone." She smiled as she nodded her head. That smile gave me great peace.

Later in the evening, we all gathered around the kitchen table. Kathy felt well enough to sit with everyone. Some came to that table with the idea of discussing sad things filled with gloom and doom from the past, but I knew in my heart that this was not the time for sad things. My sister's looming death was an inescapable fact, but that did not mean that our last time together as a family had to be sad. This was a celebration of our love for Kathy. Desperate to lighten her mood, I decided to be the comedian.

I told stories about the funny things that happened when we were kids. Like the time my brother tormented me while we were eating—one of his favorite things. He told me when I was little that if a fly landed on my plate, it would have babies and I would have to eat them. From that point on, I would scream in horror if a fly landed on my plate. He also put shreds of paper in my oatmeal and laughed when Mom made me "finish my oatmeal." I told them a variety of stories about each sibling and it got the laughs I was hoping to enjoy.

Kathy laughed until her sides began to hurt. After an hour or so, she was exhausted from the exertion of constant laughter and wanted to lie down again. In her bedroom was a huge silver-metal oxygen tank. Attached to it was a clear plastic breathing tube. When she got overtired or breathless, she would go sit in a chair in her bedroom or lay down on her bed and enjoy the almost pure oxygen flowing into her lungs. After so much laughter, she needed some oxygen.

Together, arm in arm; we walked back to her bedroom. She was still chuckling as she climbed back into bed. I tucked the covers around her neck. She smiled at me and said, "Mick you're too much!" I knew I had done the right thing. I sat beside her on the bed while she fell asleep.

Lee never called during that weekend. He knew she was dying. I felt he was responsible for so much pain in my sister's life. I was relieved that Kathy did not have to speak with him.

I kissed my dear sister goodbye. Every time I think about how long and hard she squeezed me, I still cry. When I look back on that time, I wonder what I had been thinking. I was in denial. I never believed in my heart, that she would actually die.

August 17, 2004

The phone rang. It was Mom. "She's gone, Mick."

"What? Who is gone?" I asked her.

"Kathy ... your sister is dead. She passed a little while ago. I'll call you a little later ... okay?"

I had felt it earlier that day—standing at the kitchen sink, my sister flashed into my mind. I could see her pulling into the driveway of Mom's house, to pick me up to babysit. She looked so full of life in her shag haircut and blue jeans. That is when I knew she was gone.

As I hung up the phone, I collapsed into a puddle of tears. My heart was broken. She never lived the life she should have had—her life stolen from her. Stolen by an evil man, a warlock who cared nothing for her or for anyone else. I cried for what might have been … for the happiness lost, and the joys never experienced. At that moment, I realized that evil had taken many years of our lives from us. In the end, Kathy had come back to the Lord and had found peace. That was all that mattered.

My lovely sister, Kathy, passed away peacefully, at home. Her torment was finally over.

***

I flew to Phoenix. We held a memorial service for her at a local church. Many of her personal things were on display on the altar of the church: photos, scrapbooks, photograph books. I was standing there just staring at it all when someone tapped me on the shoulder. I turned around and looked into a face I had not seen in many years. "I know your face," I told the man.

The handsome older man replied, "It's me, Mick, … Seb."

I grabbed him and hugged as hard as I could. He was the embodiment of the life she had lost so long ago. I kept thinking about Kathy's words to me. "I should never have left Seb," she told me.

Seb had been out of my life and out of Kathy's for over thirty years. We walked over to one of the old photograph books. I knew he would remember the pictures—he was in most of them. In a few of the photographs, Kathy was pregnant with Danny. Their first child. We stood and looked through the book together. Then we hugged each other again. Fighting back tears.

George Lee Lutz never bothered to attend my sister's memorial service. Frankly, I was relieved. However, he and Kathy had two girls together and George had lived with Danny, Chris, and Missy for years. Still, he could not be bothered. Perhaps he knew that no one wanted him there. I certainly did not. My brother and I had made a pact. If he showed up, we were going to throw him out.

Mercifully, he did not show his face.

Mom was heart-broken over Kathy's death. Her daughter was dead; her grandchildren left without a mother—too soon. *He* was still alive ... it was not right.

Kathy and George were married for eleven years before she divorced him. At her death, in August of 2004, they had not lived together for several years. Even though she was able to get physically free from Lee, her spirit was still in his clutches.

Lee had been an almost constant source of torment for my sister ... even to her dying breath. He had high-jacked her happiness, and in so many ways, the happiness of her children. A heart is such a heavy thing to carry and certainly not for the weak minded.

In 1990, I dedicated one of my poems, "Stance of a Warrior" to my sister, Kathy.

Stance of a Warrior

*He sharpens his two-edged sword, upon a stone
called faith.*

*Securely he has fastened the belt of truth about
his waist.*

*His helmet glimmers, polished with the promise of
salvation.*

*His breastplate is scarred, marred by arrows of
temptation.*

*Eyes reflect the certainty of what he hopes for, the
assurance of what he does not see.*

*Feet shod within the promise of peace, he takes
his stance against the enemy.*

*Fearless is he of the battle, as he stands there face
to face.*

*Heart resting fully assured, of being homeward
bound by grace.*

Kathy's war with the warlock was over. There were
no more tears, no more fear and regret. Only peace, the
peace she had longed for in life. I take comfort in knowing that she is at peace, finally without torment. I miss
her every day.

In 2006, two years after Kathy's death, George Lee
Lutz died of a heart attack. I did not attend his funeral.
He was gone. From the grave, he was powerless to hurt
our family. At least that was—and is—my hope.

No more hauntings, no more visits from demons he
had conjured from the pit of hell. No more tearful, frantic calls from my sister, in fear for her soul. No more

curses in the mail, or poisoned coffee. No more George Lee Lutz.

I'm hoping that there won't be another chapter—that I won't ever have to write a sequel …but you never know what will reach up out of the dark and grab you.

what really

happened?

What Really Happened in the Amityville House?

Although no one can know for sure what happened during those 28 days in the Amityville house, I want to include my brother's statement regarding "the day of the flies" that is chronicled in the Amityville book.

Based on the interviews given by George and Kathy on television after the event, they experienced many "poltergeist" like paranormal activity. Those stories are told in Anson's book the *Amityville Horror*.

In my opinion, Kathy had convinced herself, with the help of George, that the Amityville house was haunted. Based on my experience and knowledge of George Lutz, I believe that Lee's presence, (no matter what evil may have existed in the house before they moved in) exacerbated the strange alleged events that occurred in that house. I believed then and still believe that Lee was a warlock of the first order.

The following passive is an excerpt of one of the last conversations about Amityville that I had with my brother concerning what became known as the "day of the flies."

My brother, James Francis "Jimmy" Conners, died of cancer on October 21, 2015. He was 67 years old. Jimmy had served twenty-four years in the United States Army. Months before he died, he and I had a conversation about his visit with Kathy at the Amityville house, so many years ago. What follows is Jimmy's statement on what happened during that visit, and some of our conversation concerning Kathy and George Lee Lutz:

Jimmy's Statement

I called Kathy, to let her know I would be on Long Island, and would have a little time to visit. Carrie, my wife really wanted to see Kathy and George's new house. I wanted to see my sister and make sure she was doing all right. I was curious too, about the big old house they had just purchased in Amityville. I could only spend the day. I had to get back. The army expected me and I did not have the luxury of being late.

When we arrived at the Lutz's new house, Kathy answered the front door almost before I could knock. I took one look at Kath's face and knew something was wrong. Since her marriage to Lee, Kathy had become more and more withdrawn from her friends, and especially from the family. I asked her, 'My God, Kathy, what's wrong? Are you all right? You look terrible.'

She answered, 'No, Jimmy ... I'm fine ... really. It is great to see you and Carrie. Please come in.'

As soon as we stepped inside the house, I realized that it was alive with the constant buzzing and darting of flies. They were everywhere: on the windowsills, the drapes and furniture. They were dive-bombing counter tops. Kathy seemed oblivious to them. It was like she didn't want to see it.

She told me, 'Sorry, you two, I'm afraid the house is over run with flies. We really don't know what to do about it all.'

Next, we went into the spacious kitchen. Lee was standing beside the sink. He was dressed in jeans and a plaid shirt. He had a rolled newspaper in his hand. He was using it to swat flies. He turned quickly, said 'hello' then resumed swatting flies.

Flies were on the stove, in the window above the sink, and on the kitchen table.

Kathy looked at me and said, 'The kids are all upstairs. Let's sit in the living room? I will have the children come down and say 'hello.' They will be thrilled to see you.'

As we all headed for the living room, I grabbed a piece of newspaper from the kitchen counter, rolled it in my hands and began helping Lee smash flies. 'Mick, I swatted flies for 25 minutes ... I got SICK of doing it!'

The kids came downstairs. They were unusually quiet and pale. They really did not have much to say. I felt like something was wrong, but I did not know what it might be. After a few minutes, the kids went back upstairs. Kathy told me not to 'worry about dinner. It is already made, Jimmy,' she told me. 'All I have to do is reheat it.'

"It all seems so weird, Mick!" Jimmy told me.

Carrie helped Kathy set the table while Kathy busied herself with the meal. When the meal was ready, the kids were called and everyone sat at the table, ready to eat. Arms waved frequently to keep the ever-present flies away from the food.

When everyone finished eating, the kids went back upstairs.

Then Kathy served after-dinner 'coffee.' While we sat at the table, I got Kathy caught up on news from home. All of a sudden, Lee leaned forward, and pulled a piece of paper from his back pocket and placed it in front of me. "Jim, take a look at this. It states that you were here today and that you saw the flies in the house. If you sign it there will be some money in it for you ... later on.'

"What's this all about, Lee?' I asked him.

'Well, Jimmy, ever since we moved into the house, strange things have been happening. No one believes us. So, we thought you could be an eye-witness.'

"Mick," I glanced at the contract and looked at Kathy. She pleaded with me to sign it."

'It will help us, Jimmy,' Kathy assured me. I signed the contract and handed it back to Lee.

'Thank you, Jimmy,' Lee said as the folded the contract and put it back in his pocket. 'This will help us with something that is happening with the house.'

A few minutes later, Carrie and I said our goodbyes and left.

"You know, Mick ... I never saw that contract again and I never saw a nickel for it," Jimmy told me.

Jimmy looked at me and shook his head. I could not hide the grin on my face. "What's so funny, Mick," Jimmy asked me.

"Well Jimmy, don't you think it was a little convenient that Lee had a contract all made out for you to sign after dinner ... really?" Then he looked at me and started to laugh.

"You are right, Mick." We laughed together for a moment.

"Jimmy ... Lee probably used you more than once. Maybe it was good that you got off so easily." We laughed some more.

I told Jimmy I was going to include his statement in this book. He told me, "That's fine, Mick."

***

Evil people exist in this world. Some are attracted to places where evil has flourished in the past. This may have been the case with George and the Amityville house. I know that he had foreknowledge that the house was a "tainted" property. I had seen the newspaper clippings in his bedroom nearly a year before he purchased the house.

The untold story is that the "horror" did not begin in Amityville, and it certainly did not end when Kathy and George moved out.

epilogue

Some things are a sacred responsibility to me and speaking about this topic is certainly one of them. Humankind has questioned the subject of death from the beginning. Some in the past have lied about dying and coming back, leaving in the wake of their lies, scars upon those who tell the truth.

What you will read next is my account of my own death.

> The last thing I remember about the surgery was feeling the surgeon's scalpel make a great incision across my side and back, in the shape of a fish gill. At that second, my mind seemed to rise a few inches in front of my face as I listened to myself scream. I heard shouting in the room—then everything went black. A blackness so stark it was the absence of light—pitch black.
>
> There were no lights ... no tunnels.

I simply became aware of where I was. I was lying on my back, in a row of other people. Like a furrowed field, there were rows and rows of people. I can only guess and say there were hundreds of people. Each row was separated by about five feet. Every row the same ... bodies lined up, flat on their backs, shoulder to shoulder.

The Lord Jesus Christ was passing down each row. When He began his slow walk down my row, He came to be in front of me. He said in a very still, quiet voice, "Get up, now."

I instantly began rushing forward. It was like speeding through time and space in a roller coaster. The more forward I was propelled—the colder it became. It was a death cold. When I finished rushing forward, I opened my eyes and saw that I was lying on a metal table in the hospital morgue.

The Lord had sent me back. I can only refer to where I had been as a Gathering Place. Now, decades later, I still call it a Gathering Place. There are many others just like me out there. Others who have also been "sent back." Why? Only the Lord can answer that question.

I would like to point out that there were no babies or no children in the Gathering Place. I am of the concrete belief that the innocent go directly into the arms of the Lord.

I hope that knowledge may be a comfort to someone who may wonder what happened to a child that passed from this life into the next.

When I was young, a neighbor girl, five years old, lived at the end of our block. One day, while playing, a speeding car ran over her. As her mother kneeled beside her body waiting for help to arrive, the child looked into her mother's eyes and said, "Mommy, I see the angels coming." Those were her last words. Those words were the topic of discussion for days after her accident. What happened? Did she really see an angel coming for her? I believe that she did. My own near-death experience supports that belief.

Everyday my scars remind me of how much the Lord has carried me through in times of trouble. I suppose it is the same for others as well. There are many different things that people believe in, but I can assure of this, when your moment comes … you are going to meet the Lord.

afterward

Many of the people involved in this story have died in the intervening years as I have kept my silence for forty years. The events depicted in this book are true, based on my recollections of events, conversations, and observations. Kathy Lutz was my sister and I love and miss her. How much she knew of the warlock's hoax, I could not say for sure. We never discussed it. However, I hope you will realize from reading this book how completely George Lee Lutz controlled my sister.

Kathy regretted ever marrying him. She told me that. Whether she regretted any of the things she said in interviews she gave concerning the "Amityville House," I cannot know. She was never comfortable discussing those things with me.

George Lutz brought significant pain to me, my sister, my mother, and to my niece and nephews. That fact is undeniable. Even Harry, the dog, was not exempt from his formidable anger.

Evil is with us. It lives amongst us. The "sociopath next door" may be suffering from more than mental disease—there *is* true evil in this world. When evil is visited upon the souls of men, those souls become a putrid thing that reeks harm, casts spells, manipulates, hurts, hunts, stalks, and sometimes … kills.

It is my belief that George Lee Lutz was a man guided by evil influences, a man in concert with darkness. Perhaps that is why, when he wanted to perpetrate a hoax, he chose a house that had borne witness to the murder of six innocent people. Was this a case of evil attracting evil?

To this day, long after Lutz's death on May 8, 2006, his legacy of fear and pain lives on … and so too, do the stories about the "Amityville house."

I believe that evil never dies, but transcends to the "next"—Satan recycles too.

Edmund Burke once said, "The only thing necessary for the triumph of evil is for good men to do nothing." The forces of darkness are attracted to the light and consumed with destroying it. The mission of evil is to inflict, destroy, manipulate, and control the hearts and minds of humankind. Evil hates humankind and fear is its main weapon. What you allow to influence your mind is a lethal choice in the battle for your soul—the unseen war that rages around each of us every day. Be vigilant and guard your heart. Stand, and do not waver.

In some way, I hope that this story can chase away the darkness for those who may be experiencing its oppression.

about the author

Micky Sexton is an award-winning poet. Micky is a native New Yorker. She grew up on Long Island.

She began writing poetry in 1989. Sexton won Poet of Merit and Poetic Achievement awards in 1989. That same year she published four poems in the American Poetry Anthology, Vol IX. Her poems, published in *Great Poems of the Western World II*, the *Swing of Spring*, *Pegasus*, and *Publisher's Choice* have won several Golden Poet awards from the World of Poetry.

"I must admit, I never read much poetry before I began to publish most of my work," Sexton says.

Over the years, her life has been "impacted by the occult" which led to the writing of this book, *Amityville-My Sister's Keeper: A Story of Death, Deception and the Occult.* The book is Sexton's recollections of events and conversations with her sister, Kathy Lutz and her brother-in-law, George Lee Lutz.

This is her first full-length book. It reveals the backstory of George and Kathy Lutz before, during, and after they spent their infamous "28 days" in the Amityville House. After forty years of silence, Sexton says that she feels a great weight has lifted from her shoulders.

"Finally," says Sexton, "I can tell people what really happened to my sister and her children."

Sexton is engaged and living in Nevada.

a final note

Although I have been through terrible trials in my life, my Irish sense of humor says that at least my life has never been boring. On the serious side, I hope that none of these horrors ever happens to anyone else.

Micky Sexton

TO LEARN MORE AND STAY CONNECTED WITH MICKY
To connect with Micky, or to read her blog, visit her website at www.MickySexton.com.

Made in the USA
Coppell, TX
01 February 2024

28492862R00135